Justice as Enlightenment and Morality

Justice as Enlightenment and Morality

Dr. Ghazala Rizvi

GenNext Publication

First Published, 2020

Published by

GenNext Publication
5, Ansari Road
Daryaganj, New Delhi-110002
Phone: 9811692060
E-mail: gennextpublication@hotmail.com

Printed at: G. Print Process, Delhi.

Cataloging in Publication Data—DK
Courtesy: D.K. Agencies (P) Ltd. <docinfo@dkagencies.com>

Rizvi, Ghazala, 1990- **author.**
Justice as enlightenment and morality / Dr. Ghazala Rizvi.
pages cm
Includes bibliographical references.
ISBN 9789353242923
"An Imprint of Kalpaz Publication"

1. Kant, Immanuel, 1724-1804—Ethics. 2. Justice. 3. Enlightenment. 4. Law—Philosophy. I. Title.

LCC B2799.J87R59 2020 | DDC 193 23

Contents

Introduction

I, in the present book, shall discuss enlightenment rationality and morality in the concept of justice. Justice is a concept, which deals with the fact that people should be treated fairly and impartially concerning their rights, freedom, need and choices. It is primarily concerned with the proper ordering of things which includes equitable distribution of social opportunities such as resources, goods, services and deterrence of crime and punishment within a society. Its main concern is the availability of equal social opportunities for the development of personality to all the people in the society without any discrimination on the basis of caste, color, sex or race. As a concept it has been subject to philosophical debates on moral, legal, religious and human rights issues throughout history. The diversity of its connotation makes it difficult to lay down the precise meaning of justice. It is dynamic in nature and its implication varies from time to time and situation to situation. The overall system of society has many dimensions like legal, political, economic, and social. So the concept of justice can be looked at from all these angles.

The concept of justice has been analysed differently by philosophers at different ages and it changes from time to time depending upon the conditions and circumstances prevailing in each age. Historically, Plato was the first philosopher who could give a systematic account of justice. In *Republic,* Plato's goal of whole discussion is to define justice. In Plato's view, justice is to have harmonious relations amongst the citizens and the state. A just society shall consist of just persons. For Plato, justice covers both the just person and the just city state. Justice consists in having and doing one's own duty. Everybody should mind his/her own business, i.e., that one should do the one job for which he is naturally best fitted and should not try to indulge in anyone else's job. In *Republic*, Plato's Socrates argues that justice is the harmony of the soul and the efficient functioning of a community based on contract. Plato makes the analogy of soul and state. According to Plato, "a person's soul has three parts - reason, desire and motive"[1]. Similarly, the State has three parts - the rulers,soldiersand the workers. Plato says, "A city is just when its three natural constituents or capacities are each doing their job and it was self- disciplined, brave and wise in virtue of certain other states and dispositions of those constituents"[2].

On Plato's account, desire driven persons are workers, spirit driven persons are soldiers and reason driven persons are rulers. Ifa man is controlled by reason, with spirit and desire properly subordinated, he will act in a just manner. However, if a man is controlled by desire, or even spirit, he will act in an unjust manner. Just person is at peace with himself because his/her soul is well ordered; the unjust person is miserable because his soul is divided and disordered. And the proper order of the soul is for it to be governed by knowledge of the Good. Therefore, just person is on whose soul is guided by the vision of good and whose reason governs passion.

Carrying it further on the discussion of justice, Aristotle in Book V of *The NichomacheanEthics*, discusses the concept of justice. He holds that "In justice is summed up the whole of virtue. It is complete virtue in the fullest sense, because it is the active exercise of complete virtue; and it is complete because its possessor can exercise it in relation to other person and not only by himself".[3]Aristotle argues that justice as a virtue must be something complete, that is not desired for some further end. So it seems that the virtue is the most complete virtue which is pursued wholly for itself. Aristotle claims that the most complete virtue is that which is intrinsically valuable. Aristotle proposes two conceptions of justice – general and particular. A general conception of justice is lawfulness where justice refers to what is fair and equal. Further, Aristotle divides particular conception of justice into distributive and certificatory. Distributive justice is concerned with what people deserve or else what one has the right to get. Aristotle linked the notion of distributive justice - offices and wealth, rewards and dues with the idea of proportionate equality, which in turn, connected to a theory of just rewards or equal shares according to the merit of its recipients. According to Aristotle, "what is just is what is proportional, and what is unjust is what violates the proportion".[4] Thus, Aristotle's notion of justice deals with good judgment and sense of fairness.

In the modern times, there are various notions of justice. For instance, *Utilitarianism* is a form of consequentialism where justice is based on the maximization of usefulness. Utilitarian tradition of justice requires the maximization of the total or average welfare across all relevant individuals. Thus, utilitarian tradition of justice is based on welfare maximization where some individuals are used as a means for the good of others. Mill's *Utilitarianism* is a form of consequentialism where the moral worth of an action is determined by its outcome.According to Mill,

> Justice is not as fundamental as we often think. Rather, it is derived from the more basic standard of rightness, i.e., consequentialism: what is right is what has the best consequences (usually measured by the total or average welfare caused). So, the proper principles of justice are those which tend to have the best consequences[5].

For Mill, justice is derived from the basic standard of rightness implies what is right is what has the best consequences. The proper principles of justice are those which tend to have the best consequences. In this way the principle of utility introduces system into our judgments of justice.

There are various kinds of justice, namely, retributive, restorative, and distributive. The retributive justice regulates punishment as an act of justice. The act of punishment is to defend the supremacy and authority of the moral law and to do justice. It is demanded by the sense of justice. Restorative justice is concerned with the importance of role of crime victims and community members through more active involvement in the justice process by restoring the emotional and material losses of victims, and provides a range of opportunities for dialogue, negotiation, and problem solving. It encourages the victim and the offender to be directly involved in resolving any conflict through dialogue and negotiation. Distributive justice deals with the proper allocation of things and social opportunities that include freedom, rights, liberty, wealth, power, reward, and self- respect.

Though the concept of justice has been in debate for centuries, it may not be possible for me to go into all the details of these theories of justice evolved at different stages of the social development. However, I am not going to discuss about the above philosopher's and their conception of justice. My concern is to see how they have apprehended the conception of justice.

In the European modernity, it is the enlightenment that has played the most important role in formulating the notion of justice on the basis of the autonomy of the individuals in the civil and democratic society. It is the early enlightenment that has played most important role in making a society just by criticizing king's special right. It is the early enlightenment in especially with reference to John Locke and Rousseau that tried to establish a just society. It is related to the metaphysical, epistemological and moral doctrines of Locke's philosophy and brings out its influences on social contract, human rights and toleration which underlie the basis of his individualism and justice.

Early enlightenment thinkers were Thomas Hobbes, John Locke and Jean- Jacques Rousseau who adopted the method of social contract to repudiate feudal monarchy and aristocracy by using the natural right that is freedom to enter into civil society to protect their natural rights especially right to life, liberty and property. Hobbes' social contract was not mature because he focused on authoritarian regime that could deliver justice. It was John Locke whose liberal and anti-authoritarian theory of the state led to the overthrow of the system of absolute monarchy. Locke criticized Robert Filmer's views in *Patriarcha or The Natural Power of Kings* that a king's authority was vested in him or her by God, that such authority was absolute, and therefore that the basis of political obligation lay in our obligation to obey God absolutely"[6]. Locke repudiated king's divine rights in his *First Treatise of Government.* He denied thatking has any special power. There is no divine right of King to rule human beings and God did not appoint Adam and his decedents to rule over the world. In this way Locke has repudiated king's hereditary right and states that every man has a natural right that is right to life, liberty and property. Locke's social contract was sufficient to overthrow authoritarian regime completely. It is the natural right to enter into social contract to form civil society in which natural right i.e. right to life, freedom and property ate protected by the government established to enforce laws protecting rights and its related disputes. Justice lies in protecting the rights of the individuals.

Rousseau also applied social contract approach in the form of general will i.e. will of majority. Rousseau's concept of general will is not merely the sum of all the individual wills that enter into the social contract but the will of all should give consent. In this way by entering into the original agreement confirmed to seek to consensus regarding the welfare of all and this was the vision underlying justice.

Early enlightenment has emphasized on the principles of freedom, equality, and right to all individuals and justice is meant to safeguard those principles. Justice is the universal norm that enables us to assess the fairness in terms of rights and freedom to being just individuals.

There is, however, a lack of sufficiently broad, accurate, comprehensible and useable definition of the early enlightenment.

> Part of the reason of this lack is that during enlightenment there have been complex and quite often contradictory views on such issues as democracy, modernity, secularism, religion and scientific knowledge etc. It is very difficult to provide one definition as the definition of the enlightenment which fits all the men usually assumed to belong to it. Generally among the enlightenment thinkers we have Voltaire, Rousseau, Hume, Condorcet and others[7].

The views and arguments of early enlightenment thinkers were complex and contradictory. I am however not concerned with their specific philosophical systems, their mutual agreements and disagreements. I am basically concerned with the concept of justice as the key concept of the enlightenment.

The stage of enlightenment was the beginning of a just society where individuals were free to pursue natural rights, happiness, liberty, equality and justice. During this time great changes occurred in scientific thought and exploration. New ideas filled the horizon and man was eager to explore these ideas freely. It also brought about a great change in the social relationship because at this time, reason, rationality, freedom, equality, justice became the central part of human affairs. Man began to embrace an exaggerated belief in the perfection of humanity based on reason, clear thinking. They happily left the medieval extremism of mysticism and superstitions and they changed their opinion to the other extremes of reason, rationality, science and technology.

The advancement in science in the form of Copernicus revolution also contributed in shaping the thoughts of enlightenment rationality. As a matter of fact, Kant's views on justice are greatly influenced by the enlightenment movement of the time. Enlightenment rationality is the stage at which the human beings departs from his self- incurred habits and is able to use one's own understanding without the guidance of another. In other words, it is the point at which a human being recognizes his or her own autonomy. It develops reason to the extent that it becomes autonomous and gets rid of restraints from tradition and authority. The way to enlightenment is not to seek a mentor or authority in thinking, willing and feeling. Freedom and maturity has been at the center of enlightenment. In enlightenment, freedom plays an important role because freedom makes public use of one's own reason in all matters. Kant says, public use of reason must always be free and it alone can bring about enlightenment among men, while private use of reason can be restricted.

In formulating the theory of justice in Kantian perspective, enlightenment rationality has played an important role because it is the stage at which human being recognizes his or her freedom, rationality, rights, autonomy and sovereignty. Kant's central concept and his vision of justice revolve around the idea of individual freedom, autonomy, equality, right, and sovereignty and his principle of justice is meant to regulate and safeguard individual liberty, right on the basis of moral law that ought to be universalized. Autonomy is one of the supreme principles of justice in Kant's view. For Kant,

> Autonomy of the will is that property of it by which it is a law to itself (independent of any property of the object of its volition). The principle of autonomy then is; always to choose that the same volition shall comprehend the maxim of our choice as a universal law[8].

Autonomy is possible only if the will is guided by the supreme principle of morality that he called the 'categorical imperative'. Kant views this imperative as the product of reason and human beings as rational agents are "autonomous," or have the capacity for moral self-government. Autonomy helps in impartial decision making. When we are autonomous then only we can act in just manner for ourselves and others. For instance, autonomous beings can set their own standards of conduct, as distinct from the demands made by their desires, and are able to decide and act on these standards that contribute in making a principle of justice.

For Kant, freedom is a universal concept and it should be universally applied to every human being. Freedom is a necessary presupposition of all action as well as of all thinking. Freedom, however, is a complex concept throughout Kant's philosophy. "Within Kant's moral theory there are two main types of freedom: inner and outer freedom"[9]. Inner freedom is the primary subject of Kant's ethical theory while external freedom is the primary subject of Kant's theory of justice. External freedom in the most general sense is independence of constraints imposed by others. From normative perspective, it is divided into two further categories; rightful external freedom and lawless or wild external freedom. The rightful external freedom is freedom of action circumscribed by law of justice. On the other hand, the lawless freedom is the unrestricted anarchic liberty of the state of nature. The purpose of justice for Kant is to distinguish right from lawless external freedom and to determine that which makes rightful freedom possible.

The first principle of enlightenment and justice is the rule of civil liberty described by Kant as the principle of freedom of every member of a society as a human being. The purpose of this rule is to define an area of personal liberty within which individuals are free to act as they wish. In Kant's view, human beings are essentially choice making being. To be free as a human being is to possess freedom of choice. But principle of civil liberty is a principle of justice and justice is concerned with external freedom. So the freedom of choice required by this principle must be external freedom of choice. In this way all members of society are equally human in the sense that all share equally in the capacity for free choice. Hence, Kant clearly meant that external freedom of choice must be distributed equally among all individuals.

Kant defines Justice as "the aggregate of those conditions under which will of one person can be conjoined with the will of another in accordance with a universal law of freedom"[10]. From the above passage it is clear that there are three essential characteristics of Kant's conception of justice. First, justice applies to only external relation between individuals in so far as their action may affect each other directly or indirectly. Secondly, it is not concerned with the wishes or desire of an individual but solely with the relationship of will to another person's will. Thirdly, it deals only with the form of the relations between the will in so far as they are regarded as free. Synthesizing these three characteristics, Kant reaches to his definition of universal justice.

Kant's enlightenment philosophy is preoccupied with the concept of a 'just man' who has come out of his immaturity by using his own reason securing the maximum set of liberty, equality, rights and autonomy that can be consistently enjoyed by all. The concept of right plays an important role in Kant's justice. Freedom is the only original right belonging to each man. The freedom of each man's will enables to assist side by side with the freedom of very other man in accordance with right. We can then suppose that when Kant develops freedom as the only original right of man and proposes to limit that freedom in the case of each individual solely by the demand for an equal freedom on the part of all the other individuals, it is evidently clear that for Kant an action would be contrary to right if it interferes with the formal freedom of one's neighbour.

Justice presupposes equality of rights of people and it is a kind of impartiality. It is a matter of securing the maximum set of equal rights that can be consistently enjoyed by all. Rights of man include, right to life, liberty, property and pursuit of happiness and these are the moral foundations of a just socio-political order. Kant believed that the foundation of rights of man rests in purely abstract reason able to derive absolute, unchanging, universal principles. In Kant's view, the person who lives out the reciprocal rights and duties in a society follows the only possible path to freedom. By freedom, Kant meant objective freedom of the truly human beings who is free when he gladly wills to fallow the laws of his own rational soul and the moral order of cosmos; freedom did not mean the subjective freedom of the creature who, driven by desire for pleasure feels free only when able to do whatever he wants. Kant view on rights of man is the most essential basis for the modern concept of human rights in which each individuals has a right to just treatment and reciprocal responsibility to ensure justice for others. The Kantian conception of justice has been deduced from his morality. Kant says,

> act externally so that free exercise of your personal wills could be brought under general law together with the freedom of everyone- consummates the separation between law and justice on the one hand as concerned only with external behaviour, morality on the other hand as concerned with inner life.[11]

This definition shows that justice and morality are inseparable from each other. Both are like the two sides of same coin, one is based on external life other is based on inner life. Morality and justice are interrelated concepts. Morality deals with inner sense while justice deals about external behaviour of individual.

For Kant, justice is a moral concept in treating parties equally, that is, according to general principle that binds all rational beings into one law called categorical imperative. It deals with all principles of justice and moral statements and should be deduced from general law which apply to everyone under all circumstances. There should be no occasion under which an exception of injustice is made.

Justice demands that people should be treated equally as an end in themselves rather than as a means to some other end. This view would promote equality and justice, because the first duty of justice is to never treat people as a means to one's own ends. But treating a person as an end themselves is to do more than respect this duty and it is also to assist them in achieving their moral lawful ends. It shows that act as if your maxims would harmonize with the kingdom of ends. This means that the action should be consistent and universal so that people are treated as end in themselves. It is a harmony of ends in that its members act only on maxims that can meet everyone's consent and they respect one another as a rational self-determining agent. The kingdom of ends promotes a just society or an idea of intelligible world wherein every individual becomes enlightened so that we would live in enlightened age rather an age of enlightenment that's what Kant's vision on justice was.

Kant's enlightenment ingredient such as human right, tolerance, autonomy, and public and private reason helps to transform humanity from incurred immaturity to become autonomous and sovereign. It is the enlightenment rationality which makes people autonomous and sovereign being. The autonomous beings can act on good will which can coexist with every one's action so that it becomes the universal law of morality and justice.The value of a good will cannot secure certain valuable ends whether for our own or for others. Indeed, it is good under any condition; its goodness must not depend on any particular conditions. In Kant's terms, a good will underlies the vision of just will whose decisions are wholly determined by moral demands or by the moral law.

In Kant's view a maxim is always good if it is compatible with universal principle of morality. His sense of justice bring out from the single principle of morality that categorical imperative which states that each and every individual should treated equal to each other in terms of freedom, right, autonomy, and other social opportunities. His sense of justice demands that people should be treated equally as an end in themselves in terms of social and enlightenment opportunities. For Kant, the principle of justice ought to underpin equality for

Now Kantian justice concerns about the protection of individual freedom, rights, autonomy in equality for all persons regardless of any differences like caste, colour, sex and race. Kant believed that it is the institutions which forbid any kind of inequality and deliver impartial justice. That's why his sense of justice lies in the method of social contract to form a state by a process of mutual consent and abide by common rules and accept certain duties to tolerate and protect themselves from any inequality and injustices. A just state in the form of Kingdom of ends would be possible by enlightened being and their principle of categorical imperative which fulfils the condition of universality and end in itself only by entering into an agreement upon by those autonomous being. In Kant, justice is possible with contract because it is one of the important tools to evaluate the formulated principle is either just or unjust for the sake of humanity.

The methodology of this proposed study would be normative. The normative aspects of my approach has a reference to the consideration of the nature of an ideal or standard on the basis of which an action or a conduct is pronounced to be just or unjust, right or wrong, good or bad. I will also take up historical-hermeneutic method to understand the development from early enlightenment to its mature formulation in Kant.

I shall divide my dissertation primarily into three chapters besides Introduction and Conclusion. In Chapter-I, I shall discuss the early enlightenment that helps in developing reason to the extent that it becomes autonomous and gets rid of traditions, repudiates monarch's divine rights and introduces natural rights that are right to life, liberty and property for the individuals to make society just and peaceful. Further the notion of rights, toleration and social contract in the philosophy John Locke and the concept of General Will in Rousseau have been discussed. Finally I will argue that justice has evolved out of the above normative notions.

In Chapter-II, I shall discuss Kant's enlightenment rationality and moralities which are complementary to each other will be discussed. Kant's enlightenment rationality helps to come out from immaturity to maturity by the application of one's own understanding without authority to make people sovereign and acquire the image of just man. Kant's enlightenment rationality gives universal freedom along with related concepts namely human rights, autonomy and sovereignty, public and private reason. It is complemented with morality which gives the concept of free will, categorical imperative and good will to substantiate the notion of justice.

In Chapter- III, I will discuss Kant's concept of justice based on individual freedom, equality and right. This will followed by the social contract or social agreement in terms of public reason. There will be an attempt to proper public consent or social agreement or social contract to protect individual freedom, rights, autonomy etc. then justice will prevail. It will also explain justice as an institution because people can make an agreement to enter into a civil society which safeguard our freedom, right, tolerance, autonomy and private and public right in case of disputes and violation. By the method of social contract, justice can be given. I will show that justice is always practice in institutions where certain norms in the form of terms and conditions are applied.

Last but not the least concern of this work is to reach to the enlightened age rather the age of enlightenment; this is what Kant's dream was. The sole aim of Kant's justice to provide equal opportunities to each and every individual so that everyone can become enlightened and moral; therefore they construct the maxim which formulates the universal principle of justice. In Kant's sense of justice, enlightenment and morality both inculcate a habit and duty of individuals to think boldly and use their own understanding and become autonomous, tolerance of others right, freedom to use public and private reason. This is where justice according to Kant inheres.

Notes

1. Plato, *Republic.* p. 207.
2. *Ibid.,* p. 209.
3. Aristotle, *Nichomachean Ethics*, p. 115.
4. *Ibid.,* p. 120.
5. Mill, Utilitarianism *on Liberty and Other Essays.* p. 5.
6. Locke, *First Treatise on Civil Government*. p. 28.
7. Singh. *Freedom and Causation with Special Reference to Hegel's Overcoming of Kant*. p. 21.
8. Kant. *Fundamental Principle of the Metaphysic of Ethics*. p. 71.
9. Kant. *Doctrine of Virtue*. p. 213.
10. Rosen. *Kant's Theory of Justice.* p. 75.
11. Kamenka. *Justice*. p. 21.

Chapter - 1

Status of Justice in the Early Enlightenment Rationality

In the present chapter, I shall discuss the philosophical underpinnings of the early Enlightenment Rationality especially with reference to John Locke and Jean-Jacques Rousseau. I will develop the epistemological and ethical doctrines of Locke's philosophy and bring out its influences on justice, human rights and toleration and Rousseau's doctrine of 'general will' in formulating the principle of justice based on social contract. Locke understands of justice rests on his epistemology. On Locke's view, the concept of justice begins with the sensation and a posteriori ideas in epistemology. For Locke, epistemology is one of the important tools to know about the ethical doctrine of justice. It helps us to know how to make our society just by using experience rather than reason only. It is the epistemology which gives the idea of justice, toleration, human right, and fraternity based on social contract among its citizens.

Locke's epistemological basis on sense experience influenced enlightenment philosophers. In the Enlightenment period, the notion of liberal sense of justice emerged. Enlightenment and so called liberal sense of justice begins with the struggle against monarchy and hereditary privileges. Locke and other enlightenment philosophers tried to replace monarchy with the help of notion of social contract. Social contract is based on individual's natural rights such as right to life, liberty and property. With the social contract approach, liberalism begins.

The notion of justice in liberalism is based on the institutional approach rather than authoritarian regime of king. It is the institution which protects natural rights of individuals to maintain justice. Status of justice in institutional approach repudiates all discrimination between human beings on the ground of individual's religion, race, caste, creed, sex, language, culture etc. and treat everyone with equal dignity and moral worth of all beings. The function of justice in liberalism is to regulate the mutual toleration between individuals and groups with social contract. Here the quest of justice should aim at evolving reasonable rules on human rights, toleration and it should be applied impartially to all. Freedom of the contract is the backbone of justice in liberalism.

Rousseau's notion of 'General Will' in the social contract plays a very important role in maintaining justice. Rousseau's 'general will' means the *will of all* and not of the certain individual. Rousseau's 'general will' advocates a social contract through which each individual gives up his right to control his life in exchange for an equal voice in setting the ground rules of society based on a proper and common agreement or total union. He appeals to the people to surrender their individual rights to a new moral and collective body with one will he calls the 'general will' of the society. Rousseau, put simply generality or general will has both procedural and substantive components in formulating the notion of justice. His conception of justice is based on the idea of general will.

In order to organise my discussion, I have divided my chapter into three parts. In Part I, I will develop Locke's criticism of rationalist theory of innate ideas and his formulation of empiricist theory of knowledge, dualism and freedom. In Part II, I will develop the notion of justice in the liberalism of Locke. In Part III, I will discuss Rousseau on Justice in General Will.

Part - I

Locke's Criticism of Innate Ideas and his Formulation of Empiricist Theory of knowledge

John Locke's epistemological position is based on the role of sensation in human knowledge. Locke criticizes rationalist theory of innate ideas of Descartes. His contention is that sensation and reflection are the source of knowledge, not the reason only and exclusively. Locke writes in his book, *An Essay Concerning Human Understanding*, "No innate principle in the mind and universal consent proves anything innate. If it were true in matter of fact that there were certain truths wherein all mankind agreed, it would not prove them innate"[1]. It is false that reason discover innate ideas.

> How can men think the use of reason necessary to discover principles that are innate, when reason is nothing else but the faculty of deducing unknown truths from principles or propositions that are already known? That certainly can never be thought innate which we have need of reason to make the understanding see what is originally engrave in it[2].

The human mind attains several truths step by step. In the beginning, mind is like a *tabula rasa*. The senses at first let in particular ideas. The mind by degree grows familiar with some of them, and they are lodged in the memory. Afterwards the mind gradually proceeds farther, abstracts them, and by degrees learns the use of general names. In this manner the mind comes to be furnished with ideas and language, the materials about which to exercise its discursive faculty; and the use of reason becomes daily more visible, as these materials increase.

Locke writes that.

> Though the having of general ideas, and the use of general words and reason, usually grew together, yet I see not how this any way proves them innate. The knowledge of some truths, I confess, is very early in the mind; but in a way that shows them not to be innate. For, if we will observe, we shall find it still to be about ideas not innate, but acquired; it being about those first, which are imprinted by external things, with which infants have earliest to do, which make the most frequent impressions on their senses. Locke says that men have in their minds several ideas such as hardness, sweetness, thinking, motion, man, and others and by what ways and degrees they; for which I shall appeal to every one's own observation and experience[3].

This definition show that no ideas are innate rather each idea derived from some experience.

Further, he says,

> Let us then suppose the mind to be, as we say, white paper, void of all characters, without any ideas; how comes it to be furnished? Whence comes it by that vast store, which the busy and boundless fancy of man has painted on it with an almost endless variety? Whence has all the materials of reason and knowledge? To this answer, from experience; in that all our knowledge is founded, and from that it ultimately derives itself. For him, our observation, employed either about external sensible objects, or about the internal operations of our minds, perceived and reflected on by ourselves, is that which supplies our understanding with all the materials of thinking. These two are the fountains of knowledge, from which all the ideas we have[4].

Thus how we come to the conclusion that any knowledge is sufficient to prove that it is not to be innate.

On Locke's view, all men acquire knowledge through ideas and all ideas come from sensation or reflection. Locke repudiated the doctrine of innate ideas developed by Descartes. He regards human mind to be like a blank sheet on which man writes what he derives from sensations. The objects of sensation are one source of ideas and the operations of our minds are the other source of our knowledge. The causes of the sensations are the primary and the secondary qualities. The primary qualities are solidity, extension, figure, motion rest and number. These are inseparable from the material things. The secondary qualities are colour, taste, smell, sound, etc. These are partly caused by the material things and partly by the perceiving subject.

> Sensations arise in accordance with the affections of the material things by means of their primary and secondary qualities. These sensations reflected in the mind and thus simple ideas are formed. With the comparison and contrast among the simple ideas, complex ideas are formed. Our cognition, according to Locke is confined to the fields of simple and complex ideas. And our ideas are copies of things[5].

It may be pointed out that human mind, for Locke, is completely passive so far as simple ideas are concerned because it simply reflects what is given to it by the objects. So what is active in the formation of simple ideas is the object. But in the sphere of complex ideas human mind is active because it compares and contrasts the simple ideas and thus actively forms the complex ideas.

John Locke's *An Essay Concerning Human Understanding* furnishes a detailed account of his epistemology. Locke basically classifies his epistemology into three kinds; namely sensitive, intuitive and demonstrative. In Locke's formulation of sensitive knowledge, the status of sensibility is, however, one sided. This is so because Locke vindicates a material substance as something 'we know not what' this material substance is and what causes material things and events which affect our senses. But the material substance transcends the apprehension of sensibility. So there is a separation between sensibility and the material substance. For Locke, the material substance exists that we know but what it is we cannot say. We can know the material substance in terms of 'thatness', but we cannot know it in terms of its 'whatness'. Locke's material substance is something beyond the primary and secondary qualities. This is perhaps the reason why it is unknown. However, the existence of material substance beyond the primary and secondary qualities is nothing but an abstraction. In this way in sensitive knowledge, external objects cannot be known either through intuition or demonstration. Knowledge gained through the sense is called sensitive knowledge. Senses enable us to know the world and objects around us. Sense knowledge is different from knowledge gained through dreams, illusion and hallucinations. It has greater veracity than these forms of knowledge. Sense knowledge is more than mere possibility. Yet it is not ascertain as intuitive or demonstrative knowledge.

Locke's formulation of intuitive knowledge is another illustration of epistemology. For, Locke, like Descartes, mind and matter are two different substances. According to Locke,

> Mind can know its own ideas a.nd the agreement or disagreement of any of its ideas. The different clearness of our knowledge seems to me to lie in the different way of perception the mind has of the

agreement or disagreement of any of its ideas immediately by themselves without the intervention of any other…[6].

This is what Locke's calls the intuitive knowledge. For example, mind can perceives the truths, such truths as white is not black a triangle is not circle etc. Mind can perceives at the first sight of the ideas together by bare intuition without the intervention of any other ideas and this kind of knowledge is the clearest and the most certain that human being is capable of.

This part of knowledge is like bright sunshine forces itself immediately to be perceived as soon as ever the mind turns its view that way and leaves no room for doubt, but the mind is presently filled with the clear light of it. It is on this intuition that depends all the certainty and the evidence of our knowledge[7].

As for Locke, intuition is completely separate from sensibility. Consequently, there are two realms- one for sensibility and the other for intuition. Intuition gives the knowledge of the knowing self. Locke regards the knowing self as so clear and evident that it does not require any proof. However, Locke's interpretation of the knowing self is very abstract, because its nature is conceived in separation from the sensitive and intuitive knowledge. Therefore, in this type of knowledge, the mind perceives the relation between ideas without taking the assistance of other ideas. For example, the difference between the ideas of black and white, circle and triangle, two and three, are perceived immediately. Knowledge of difference between them is complete, immediate and definite. There is no need to prove it. In fact, it cannot be proved. Locke is of the opinion that the reality and proof of our knowledge depends on intuition.

In the case of demonstrative knowledge, sometimes we do not directly notice the relation between two ideas but indirectly establish a relation between the two. Such a process requires the intervention of other ideas. The intervention of other ideas helps us in reaching to certain conclusion. This is logical knowledge. Logic provides a demonstrative knowledge in which a conclusion is arrived at through reasoning. In fact, Locke treats only intuitive and demonstrative knowledge as real and definite. It is on this intuition that depend all the certainty and evidence of all our knowledge. Though Lock's theory of mind as *tabula rasa* devoid of all innate ideas which justifies the claims of scientific knowledge that is based on observation and experiment.

It is on the intuitive self that freedom is in the last analysis located. This view provided the main basis for the enlightenment. In this way Locke had become the acknowledged authority on the human mind. Locke view on

> Freedom lies on the intuitive self and it developed a confidence in the workings of human mind. This view was the champion of human subjectivity and freedom and his notion of freedom involves dualism in exactly the same way as it is in Descartes. Both Descartes and Locke regard freedom and causality as separate with no meeting transition. Despite this Cartesian influence on himself, Locke was basically a philosopher of the enlightenment[8].

Locke upheld the supremacy of scientific knowledge and attempted to reconcile science with religion. The criticism of innate ideas, religion, tradition and rise of humanism and the concept of justice are the preconditions to the emergence of freedom. The development of modern science and with it the emergences of different epistemological situations are infused approximately to the doctrine of freedom. Here, we can state that the philosophical movements of the Enlightenment are the historical determinants to the concept of freedom.

Part - II

Justice in the Liberalism of Locke

Enlightenment and the so called liberal thinkers repudiated the traditional way of authoritarian regime and establish a just society wherein individuals have autonomy, rights, freedom, equality, toleration. They bestowed the sense of autonomy, rights, toleration. Enlightenment thinkers and their ideas help in formulating the notion of justice. They took liberal position of justice and for them equality is autonomy in all matters for enhancing justice. Locke's concept of justice is based on the social contract, human rights and toleration. Locke employed the concept of the social contract theories to shares a set of core principles and assumptions that include the principle of human equality, individualism, autonomy and toleration. In social contract approach, each human being is an equal and autonomous individual means that no person has natural authority over another. Social contract approach appeals to the principle of voluntarism in explaining the origin of moral and political obligations and to the principle of consent in explaining how the autonomous individual voluntarily renounces her natural liberty to the state, thereby acquiring moral and political obligations for making a just society.

The main concern of liberal theory of justice is that justice consists in applying general rules impartially to all citizens regardless of their circumstances or differences. Justice lies in the principle of constitutionalism, that is, the concept of justice exists in constitution or rules of law. Justice is opposed to rule by a dictator's rule. Justice entails about basic individual rights, such as right to life, liberty, property, freedom of religion, freedom of expression and freedom association and so on so.

At the time of pre enlightenment our society was full of injustices and rights and privileges were in the hands of a few people. The liberal thinkers bring the enlightenment and justice by introducing the idea of human rights. Among the philosophers of liberalism, John Locke was especially known for his liberal, anti-authoritarian theory of the state. He repudiated injustice of monarch's divine rights based on the theory of social contract and developed a just society which gives human rights, toleration, equality, fraternity to every individual. Liberalism seeks to bring about justice through social contract method. The Philosophers of liberalism believed that state is an artificial institution created by social contract among the individual beings. Social contract holds that state is not a natural institution but an artificial institution invented or discovered by men for their mutual benefit and just society. In *Two Treatise of Government*, Locke writes:

> men being, as has been said, by nature all free, equal, and independent, no one can be put out of this estate and subjected to the political power of another without his own consent, which is

> done by agreeing with other men, to join and unite into a community for their comfortable, safe, and peaceable living, one amongst another, in a secure enjoyment of their properties, and a greater security against any that are not of it. This any number of men may do, because it injures not the freedom of the rest; they are left, as they were, in the liberty of the state of Nature. When any numbers of men have so consented to make one community or government, they are thereby presently incorporated, and make one body politic, wherein the majority have a right to act and conclude the rest[9].

The creation of state is intended to serve the interests of all individual and all sections of society to maintain justice. The state or institutions is the product of the will of society and it is the expression of the social justice of the common will. Liberalists believed that men are capable of organising themselves into a just society through voluntary cooperation. Justice in the society can be restored only if the authoritarian regime is abolished. Liberalism rejects all forms of divine or original rights of king and tried to provide justice in the form of natural rights and the welfare of the entire individual.

Status of the notion of justice in liberalism has remained a transitional and important subject. It aims at replacing monarchy's right by individual rights for which revolution is indispensible. For instance, Locke has tried to justify the Glorious Revolution of 1688 and he was an ardent advocate of constitutional monarchy. In fact he argued, if the monarch ever behaved in a despotic manner or unjust toward people, the people had right to remove him from the authority. Liberalists inclined towards justice and for them justice would mean maintaining the existing system with complete revolution in the form of individual autonomy, human rights, liberty, and toleration and thus they try to transform the society from kings divine right or absolute monarchy to the just society by individual rights or constitutional monarchy.

Among the philosophers of liberalism, Lockewas especially known for his liberal, anti-authoritarian theory of the state. His notion of liberal justice comes into existence after overthrow of the absolute monarchy system through social contract. He has evolved a unique methodology in the formulation of the notion of justice. This methodology is social contract. It presents a new version of the constitutional monarchy in the form of justice from the liberal point of view. Social contract treats the status of justice exists in institutions as the product of the mutual agreement of people within the society. Status of justice found in the form of human rights as expounded by Locke. For maintaining the notion of justice in liberalism, Locke rejected the theory of divine right of kings. However, Robert Filmer in his book, *Patriarcha or the Natural Power of Kings,* defended the theory of divine right of kings. Locke rejects Filmer's defence of the theory of divine right of kings. Locke writes that "His view held that a king's authority was invested in him or her by God, that such authority was absolute, and therefore that the basis of political obligation lay in our obligation to obey God absolutely"[10]. Locke has rejected the view of the absolutist argument of the patriarchal theory of divine right of monarch given by Sir Robert Filmer. Filmer argued that kings were the direct heirs of Adam. With this contention Locke repudiated king's divine rights in his *First Treatise of Government*. He argues:

> That Adam had not, either by natural right of fatherhood, or by positive donation from God, any such authority over his children, or dominion over the world, as is pretended. That if he had, his heirs, yet, had no right to it. That if his heirs had, there being no law of nature nor positive law of God that determines which is the right heir in all cases that may arise, the right of succession, and consequently of bearing rule, could not have been certainly determined[11].

Filmer and Hobbes represented departures from traditional way of thinking of authoritarian regime and maintaining the conservative position that the monarch or kings were the sovereign. and individuals must give up or conceded their rights and elects an absolute authority if the society is to survive and make just society. It is true that Hobbes rejects the early view and argued that the power ought to be shared between Parliament and the King. He also rejected Filmers's views, and at the same time he favored radical and conservative position. He was radical because he argued that political authority and its obligation are based on the individual's self-interests within the society who are equal to one another and no single individual invested with any essential authority to rule over the others. While at the same time maintained the conservative view of monarch which is supposed to be Sovereign and must be surrendered to absolute authority if society is to survive and make free from war and to be just. However, Locke was against and rejected the view points of the absolutist argument regarding absolute power of king. He denies that there is any natural social hierarchy that some individuals are born to perform subordinate functions or that we made for one another's uses. Rather he supposes that the natural state of persons involves equality of freedom and rights to enjoy it. Locke writes,

> all men are naturally in, and that is, a state of perfect freedom to order their actions, and dispose of their possessions and persons, as they think fit, within the bounds of the law of nature, without asking leave, or depending upon the will of any other man. A state also of equality, wherein all the power and jurisdiction is reciprocal, no one having more than another; there being nothing more evident, than that creatures of the same species and rank, promiscuously born to all the same advantages of nature, and the use of the same faculties, should also be equal one amongst another without subordination or subjection, unless the lord and master of them all should, by any manifest declaration of his will, set one above another, and confer on him, by an evident and clear appointment, an undoubted right to dominion and sovereignty[12].

Locke believes that all men should have freedom to choose the course of his or her life. The will of the individual shall be respected. And the state must guarantee its citizens equal power where no one should have power over the other.

Locke criticizes king's hereditary rights and states the existences of a natural law that transcends any man-made law. According to Locke, all men have three natural and basic rights, namely, right to life, liberty and property, which creates the philosophy of individualism. Locke's individualism states that each person has, in her own well-being an end of ultimate value and others have also the rights to devote themselves to the pursuit of their own well-being. An individual's ethos ought to be understood as including both a disposition to seek one's own well-being and to constrain one's pursuit out of regard for others' rights.

> Locke's political theory is individualistic as a normative theory of individual natural rights. Locke seeks to combat authoritarianism by altering the relation between admittedly powerful social forces and political rights. Locke's anthropological accounts do not depict isolated individuals whose behavior is governed by rational calculations of their interests but he acknowledges the extent to which all men are social beings and all men should get justice within the society[13].

For Locke, the sense of justice can bring once individual enter into social agreement to form the government for the protection of their natural rights to life, liberty and property. Locke focuses that if the state or government fails to deliver justice, individuals can resist it. If it still fails, they can dissolve government and eradicate injustices from the society. Pre-enlightenment society and individuals faced a lot of injustices because they were deprived from natural and fundamental rights. At that time pre enlightenment, most of the rights and power were concentrated in the hands of the people. Due to lack of these basic rights, individual became the slave to monarch. It was the enlightenment which repudiated monarch's special rights and established a society with social contract which provides rights, toleration and justice. Provision of these rights is automatically linked with the concept of social justice. Justice in liberalism bring out from the theory of natural rights. Liberalism deals about the human rights and they treat the rights of man as a self-evident truth. In other words these rights are not granted by the kings or monarch, but they come from the very nature of man or his own intrinsic being. Deprivation of individual rights is the injustice within the society. Now the question arise how to eradicate injustice and gain individual rights to maintain justice in the society. The sense of justice in the form natural rights can be possible on the basis of contract. We can acquire justice on the basis of contract through human rights, equality and toleration.

Locke says,

> When men think of themselves as organised with each other they must remember who they are. They do not make themselves, they

> do not own themselves, they do not dispose themselves, and they are the workmanship of God. They are his servants, sent into the world on his business, they are even his property. For Locke, this was a proposition of common sense, or the initial position of his work which appeals to common sense throughout and from this common sense starting point he proceeds to two inferences, that we are all free and we are all equal; free of each other, that is to say, and of equal to each other, for we are not free of God's superiority and not equal to him. If God could be shown to have given any man, or any order of men, superiority over other men, then these inferences could not be drawn[14].

This is the logical function of the *First Treatise* in Locke's work on government. Quite simply and quite literally, then men were born free in Locke's view. Locke further says "we all have the same faculties, the same natural advantages; power and jurisdiction is must and reciprocal among us. Again you do not have to accept a theology to be that this is all a matter of common sense"[15]. Now the question arises that if it is true that God leaves us free, and it is relevant to ask what positively makes us free, and in what does this freedom consist.

> Absolute freedom has no meaning, it must be defined where there is no law and there is no freedom. It is the law of nature which sets the bounds to natural freedom. Locke took up toward natural law; the law of nature is the law of reason. It is our reason which promulgates to us the law of nature and it is our reason which makes us free. We are born free, as we are rational and have liberty of acting according to our own will, never from compulsion by the will of others, is governed on the possession of reason[16].

For Locke, reason and freedom is the mode of cooperation between men, and reason is also the common bond whereby human being is united into one fellowship and societies.

Locke believed in the maintenance of justice can be possible within organised society. On Locke's view, this can be possible through rationality of perfect freedom, equal to each other, capable of rational behaviour and cooperation with each other. Locke argued from the dogmatic rationalist position that, the basis of political life is the rule of the rational man over his irrational fellows. There is no any arbitrary source of power in which one man rule over another not even a source in revelation, for divine right has already been disposed of as not proven. Now the question arise is that how is the government possible at all if there is no any divine right? He answers everyone has the executive power of the law of nature. This natural right which arises out of humanity itself, is based not simply the right of governing, but its power as well, for it is a collective power which is used against an offender even if only one man wields it. The right of governing and the power to govern is a fundamental, individual, natural right and power, set alongside that of preserving oneself and the rest of mankind. It is judicial in its nature, for it is the pronouncing and enforcing of a law which is guided by the law of reason.

The social contract has a rich history and it rejected the traditional way of thinking that divine right of king is supreme; it played an important historical role in the emergence of the idea that political authority must be derived from the consent of the governed. The tradition of social contract originated from ancient times. Since ancient times the social contract idea has been at heart of a progressive intellectual tradition that has questioned authority in all its guises. It originated among the ancients with recognition that social arrangements were not the products of nature but consent and contract. It developed through the centuries as theorist sought criteria for distinguishing just contract from unjust. The search for such criteria continues in recent attempts to apply social contact theory to any just organisation and institutions. Social contract theory is the view that persons' moral and or political obligations are dependent upon a contract or agreement among them to form the society in which they live. Socrates uses social contract argument to explain to Crito, "why he must remain in prison and accept the death penalty rather than escape because he makes an agreement to obey the laws of his country"[17]. He was morally bound to fallow the laws of his country because he makes an agreement to obey. "Socrates presents his analysis of political obligation in the form of an imaginary discussion between him and the Laws of Athens"[18]. Socrates offers an argument that rests on the notion of a social contract existing between him and the city-state of Athens and having made a mutual consent that was itself a just. Socrates says in *Crito*, "We must have experience of the manner in which we order justice and administer the State, and still remains, has entered into an implied contract that he will do as society commands"[19]. Socrates asserts that he must keep to this agreement that he has made and obeys the laws in this case by not escaping and accepting the death penalty.

The social contract theory associated with early enlightenment theory and is given its first sufficient description by Thomas Hobbes. After Hobbes, John Locke and Jean-Jacques Rousseau are the best known promoters of this influential theory to make a just society through individual consent and toleration of human rights and common welfare of all human being. Hobbes, Locke and Rousseau are the most famous social contract thinkers. Each drew quite different viewpoint on the nature of political authority and how the justice to be delivered within social institutions.

Thomas Hobbes is the foremost enlightenment thinker who expanded the idea of social contract. He wrote *Leviathan* in response to the English Civil War. In this book, he wrote that in the earliest days there was no government. Instead, those who were the strongest could take control and use their power at any time over others. Hobbes's theory was that the people mutually agreed to create a state, only giving the state enough power to provide protection of their well-beings. However, in Hobbes' theory, once the power was given to the state, the people then surrendered any right to that power. Hobbes thinks that the lives of individuals in the state of nature were solitary, poor, nasty, brutish and short, a state in which self-interest and the absence of rights and contracts prevented the 'social', or society. Life was anarchic and full of injustices. Individuals in the state of nature were apolitical and asocial. This state of nature is followed by the social contract. Hobbes's *Leviathan* rested his despotism on consent. He assumed that,

> Without the restraints of government men would be in a constant of war and insecurity. They are by nature so quarrelsome and competitive that only the strongest rule will restrain them. The choice between despotism and anarchy, and this should be apparent in every one's thinking[20].

Here the state system, which grew out of the social contract, was anarchic or without leadership. For instance, the individuals in the state of nature had been sovereigns and thus guided by self-interest and the absence of rights, so the individuals now acted in their self-interest in competition with each other. Just like the state of nature, states were thus bound to be in conflict because there was no sovereign over and above the state i.e. more powerful capable of imposing social-contract laws. The social contract gained importance when individuals came together and gave up some of their individual rights and others will also do the same. This entails the establishment of a just state. The state acts as a sovereign power to protect these rights which regulate societal justice. Society was thus no longer anarchic because political authority was based on the individuals self-interest to choose their authority with mutual consent by surrendering their rights and live themselves under the shadow of monarch who was sovereign must give up to absolute authority in the form of king or head if a society to be created and he can only do justice. Liberal tradition of justice is based on the social contract. The social contract theory of the state implies that there was a time when men lived without any recognised civil law or without the state. That's why Hobbes advocated justice in absolute monarchy.

Unlike Hobbes, Locke's status of justice gets prominence in the form of natural rights. Locke's classical liberal attitude and the philosophical articulation of moral and political individualism begins in a state of nature where all people were equal and independent, and everyone had a natural right to life, liberty, and property. According to Locke,

> In state of nature all men are naturally in, and that is a state of perfect freedom to order their actions and dispose their possessions and persons as they think fit, within the bounds of the law of nature, without asking leave or depending the will of any other man. A state is also a state of equality, wherein all the powers and jurisdictions is reciprocal[21].

He also defended the claim that men are by nature free and equal against claims that God had made all people naturally subject to a monarch as Hobbes had argued.

Locke argued that people have rights, such as the right to life, liberty, and property that have a foundation of the laws of any particular society. Now the basic question arise that why men do moves from the state of nature to a state of society? Why the people in the state of nature made a contract? The answer would be the fact that men were led to leave the state of nature and to set up a society through the mode of social contract for regulating and preserving individual rights and maintain justice in the social life.The men were made to live in a state where everyone has equal rights.As *The Second Treatise* goes on, more emphasis is laid on "the great and chief end of men uniting into common wealth and putting of themselves under Government is the preservation of individual rights"[22]. The social contract is an approach intended to explain the appropriate relationship between individuals and their terms and conditions of the institution. Social contract asserts that individuals unite into political societies by a process of mutual consent, agreeing to abide by common rules and accept corresponding duties to protect themselves. It helps in eradicating any kind of injustices, violence and other kinds of harm. Since justice is a normative term and it always applies in institutions which exists through social contract.

He further supposes that in this state of nature, there are moral laws. These laws discoverable through human reason and it are sufficient to govern many relations among people of good will. In the state of nature people were guided by their moral laws, for instance, can exchange of things with one another for mutual benefit. But since some person may not always act with good will, and since those who do may be biased towards their own cause in judging violations of the moral law, people may drive additional benefit by agreeing to positive laws and responsible judges to enforce them. This basically what Locke means by a social contract which could be the establishment of just law with the help of mutual consent. In a sense it was the mission of Locke to use the social contract approach for the restatement of ancient political ideas.

John Locke's conception of the social contract differed from that of Hobbes in several fundamental ways. In Hobbesian system, people were bound to be in conflict because of their cruel and selfish nature.

In this kind of state, there must be a sovereign king over and above the state more powerfully capable of imposing social-contract. In contrast to Hobbes, Locke's central notion was that persons in a state of nature would willingly come together to form a state where they live. The individuals have the freedom to choose their ruler. In Hobbes it was the necessity to choose an absolute authority to transform the brutal state of nature to state of justice. That's why the rational being would willingly submit themselves to absolute authority for making a just and peaceful society. For Locke, in fact the individuals in a state of nature would be bound morally or by the law of nature, not to harm each other in their lives and other rights, and people would have no security in their rights and would live in fear. Locke argued that individuals would agree to form a state that would provide a neutral judge or impartial judge to protect the lives, liberty, and property of those who lived within the society. Indeed people in the state of nature make an agreement to establish a civil society which provides justice among individuals.

According to Locke,

> The state of nature is a state of peace, good will, mutual assistance, and preservation. Men are living together according to reason. In it all men by nature are equal but I cannot support all sorts of equality. Age or virtue may give a just precedence of parts and merits may place others above the common level, and yet all this consists in equality which all men are in respect of jurisdiction or dominion one over another which was the equality I there spoke of as proper to the business in hand, but being that equal rights every man has to his natural freedom without being subjected to the will or authority of any other man[23].

Locke's arguments for the social contract and for the right of citizens to revolt against their king were enormously influential on the democratic revolutions.

In the state of nature, the natural condition of human being is a state of perfect and complete liberty to conduct one's life and free from the interference of others. Further, Locke writes:

> But if it is true that God leaves us free, that nothing in the natural order can be shown to subject one man to another even apart

from the revealed will of God. It may still be relevant to ask what positively makes us free or in what does this freedom consist. It is the law of nature which sets the bounds to natural freedom and since the law of nature is an expression of God's will. Locke says reason is the voice of God in man. The law of nature is the law of reason. It is our reason which promulgates to us the law of nature and it is our reason which makes us free. *We are born Free as we are born Rational* and the liberty of acting according to our own will, never from compulsion by the will of others but is grounded on the possession of reason[24].

On Locke's view,

> The state of nature is the basis of morality and given to us by God. The state of nature has a law of nature to govern it, which obliges every one; and reason, which is the law, teaches all mankind being equal and independent, no one ought to harm another in life, health, liberty, or possessions, for men being the all the workmanship of one omnipotent and infinite wise-maker[25].

All human beings belong equally in the eyes of God and one should prohibit from harming one another. The state of nature is the state of liberty wherein individuals recognizes the law of nature and do not harm one another. Locke argues that,

> The natural liberty of man is to be free from any superior power on earth and not to be under the will or legislative authority of man, but to have only the law of nature for his rule. The liberty of man, in society, is to be under no other legislative power, but that established, by consent, in the commonwealth; nor under the dominion of any will, or restraint of any law, but what that legislative shall enact, according to the trust put in it. Freedom then is not what Robert Filmer tells us[26].

Whereas Filmer tells us to be ruled by the divine authority of the king, Locke speaks of human liberty and freedom. Freedom is governed through rationality and morality in the state of nature. It does not mean, however, that it is a state of license: one is not freedom to do anything at all one desire, or even anything that one judges to be in one's interest. The state of nature, although a state wherein there is no civil authority or government to punish people for transgressions against laws but it is not a state without morality. Persons are assumed to be equal to one another in such a state, and therefore equally capable of discovering and being bound by the law of nature.

It is belief about the law of nature is state of freedom but in it the state of war begin among individuals when one man or king declares war by trying to make him his slave, depriving his or her basic rights and making a society full of injustices and biasedness. In the state of nature where king is the supreme authority, there is no civil power or lacks civil authority to whom men can appeal. It allows them to defend their own lives; that's why they kill those who would bring force against them and bloody war begins since once war begins it is likely to continue. As Locke says,

> This is the perfect condition of slavery, which is nothing else, but the state of war continued, between a lawful conqueror and a captive: for, if once compact enter between them, and make an agreement for a limited power on the one side, and obedience on the other, the state of war and slavery ceases, as long as the compact endures: for, as has been said, no man can, by agreement, pass over to another that which he hath not in himself, a power over his own life[27].

And this is one of the strongest reasons that men moves and abandon the state of nature by contracting together to form civil government. The reason behind civil government is the individual rights which were deprived by monarch's authority. The civil government and social system are analogous to agreements or contracts. A society makes a government and the contract that establishes it. Locke's social contract developed through social cooperation to make an institution to deliver justice to all men. Locke says once individual enters into a society through consent or contractual agreement he or she has to abide until the law and its principle being a just. The principle of consent plays an important role in any social contract theory. He says:

> Men being, as has been said, by nature, all free, equal, and independent, no one can be put out of this estate, and subjected

> to the political power of another, without his own consent. The only way whereby any one divests himself of his natural liberty, and puts on the bonds of civil society, is by agreeing with other men to join and unite into a community for their comfortable, safe, and peaceable living one amongst another, in a secure enjoyment of their properties, and a greater security against any injustices. When number of men consented to make one community or government, thereby incorporated to make one body politic, wherein the majority has a right to act and conclude the rest. For when any number of men have, by the consent of every individual, made a community, they have thereby made that community one body, with a power to act as one body, which is only by the will and determination of the majority. And thus every man, by consenting with others to make one body politic under one government, puts himself under an obligation, to every one of that society, to submit to the determination of the majority of the social agreement in any institutions for enhancing justice[28].

Social contract theory applies the concept of social consent in its description of the behavior of individuals in the state of nature as they come together in a context of consent to form social, political, and legal associations and institutions to make just.

The social contract theorists pursue two distinct objectives, firstly they employ the principle of contract to account for stable and just political and social arrangements, and they employ the principle of consent to account for de jure authority and political obligation. These two objectives are interrelated but independent of each other in the theories of social contract[29].

Therefore, social contract theories that attempt to account for political obligation and social obligation are actually composite theories comprised of a social contract through mutual consent. It is the principle of social consent that is the purpose of any institution, government and civil society to make just. For Locke, the people unanimously accepted the social contract in two ways; firstly, they agreed to join together and secondly, to accept the wishes of the majority as to the form of civil administration that will govern them and deliver justice properly. We simply institute the concept of common consent to accept majority rule to apply to all laws on institutions to deliver justice fraternity and equality to all persons within the society where they are living. The fact that a majority of us believe, in good faith, that a certain course of action is best for the community and judgments of the majority are deliver from the social policy of rationality and justice.

For Locke, sense of justice can bring once individuals enter into society from state of nature to civil society through agreement to attain natural rights. Justice in liberalism lies in the human rights and the provision of this is automatically linked with the concept of toleration. Liberalism formulates the notion of justice by criticizing special rights of king and replaced it through natural rights to enter into contract. In this way Locke has brought about human rights and sense of toleration in formulating the notion of justice in society.

Locke's sense of toleration develops the concept of normative justice. It is rights centric which states that one should tolerates others right and it should be reciprocal. It regulates human affairs in accordance with the principle of human rights, human goods and human bonds. The sense of toleration helps in recognising others and this is evident in Locke's social contract. When men enter into the society based on the mutual contract for the establishment and preservation of natural rights, it naturally fallows the principle of toleration. Without the principle of toleration a society cannot be a just society. For instance, in the society certain freedoms are recognised as a contract among individuals so that they may live peacefully within a society. The sense of justice would come if people will leave peacefully and tolerate one another's way of life. Monique Deveaux says, "Toleration, both historically and today, refers to the principle and practice of non-interference. A person or institution exercises tolerance by refraining from interfering with, and/or by extending a kind of permission to, practices or beliefs with which they disagree"[30].

The sense of toleration define by saying that toleration as a set of social or political practices of the acceptance of pain .The term toleration generally refers to the conditional acceptance of or non-interference of beliefs, actions or practices of others, in which one considers to be wrong but still tolerate. For instance, there are many contexts in which we speak of a person or an institution as being tolerant, parents tolerate certain behavior of their children, a friend tolerates the weaknesses of another, a monarch tolerates dissent, a church tolerates homosexuality, a state tolerates a minority religion, a society tolerates deviant behavior. Due to social agreement the sense toleration we develop in society and community which would promote peaceful, equal and just life of every individual being. It also helps to establishes democratic life which enhances person's liberties, rights and practices and promotes justice. The sense of toleration developed the concept of justice by setting human affairs in accordance with the principle of human rights and human bonds.

Locke being an outspoken supporter of equality of natural rights of man articulated that every government's purpose is to secure these rights for maintaining justice in the social order. Being social contractarian, he believed that the legitimacy of government based on consent and agreement from its citizens must be given on the basis of equality. Locke's view of equality was not limited to the political and social realm of toleration but also promoted religious toleration. He supported general toleration of alternative religious beliefs. In *Letter Concerning Toleration*, he develops sense of toleration in several lines of arguments to establish the religious and political spheres. He argues that government should not use force to try to bring people to the true religion. The religious societies are voluntary community that have no right to use coercive power over their own members or those outside their group. In *A Letter on Toleration,* he says,

> Religious toleration claims that my writing has freed men from all dominion over the one another in matters of religion. This dominion, prevalent in one form or another throughout seventieth century, he had included a variety of attempts on the part of church and the state to enforce religious uniformity and punish dissent. Locke maintained that instead of fostering sincere piety, these efforts furnished limitless occasion for discords and wars ....rapines, slaughters, and.....hatreds[31].

On Locke's view, much of the religious turmoil during his time was attributed to the influence of certain doctrines sanctioning religious persecution because of the close alliance between church and the state.

Locke argues that religious persecution by the state is unjust and that the use of force to get people to hold certain beliefs is illegitimate. The coercive attitude of the state and church generates turmoil and that religion should be treated as a purely private and individual matter. The separation between church and state should be necessary and create a secular state which provides peace, harmony, order, and safety to every individual in the contract. Every religion and their followers are free and voluntary to form a community for the public worship of God according to its own unique cultural heritage and his will. Every individual must have the right to join and practice any religious doctrine. The government force can protect life and property of every individual but it cannot persuade one's conscience because eternal salvation cannot be forwarded through coercive measures. In this way, his idea of religious freedom and social toleration in terms of religion establish to a secular civil society which promotes harmony and justice. Locke's views on tolerations shaped the liberal theory of justice emphasising the need to separate religion from state and church.

Locke's conception of social contract, rights, toleration, equality and freedom provides a powerful tool for the just political arrangement. It is the job of political arrangement to provide each and every person with what they need such as equal rights, freedom, dignity and the right to choose a government. In formulating the status of justice in Locke, social contract I think was the very powerful approach. This approach was inspired by the background of the unjust society in the form of monarch's hereditary privileges. It was the time where all opportunities were distributed unequally to people according the class and their inherited status. Therefore, Locke's principle of toleration states that each and every individual must be treated with equal dignity and have equal opportunity wherein every man whatever their race or religion may be, they must live in harmoniously and peacefully.

Thus, Locke's principle of justice is that once the civil society is established through social contract automatically preserves autonomy, human rights, toleration. In this way Locke has brought about the right of social contract, human rights and toleration within the society to make a just society. Locke tried to establish an equal society through the method of social contract and to maintain individual rights, equality, and toleration. His status of justice represents a synthesis of the principle of autonomy, individualism, equability, liberty and toleration. He analysed the principle of justice which deals with greater autonomy, liberty, human rights, toleration and fraternity. Justice in early enlightenment era prevailed through the social agreement which asserts equality for all. It was against any kind of biasedness. Everyone must be treated equal irrespective of religion, race, caste, and ethnicity. Once individuals have equal opportunity, they enter into society from the state of nature to civil society by the contract to preserve their natural rights to life, liberty and property. Liberalism formulates the notion of justice by criticizing absolute rights of king and replaced it through natural rights of every individual. It consist in the human rights and the toleration and acceptance of others rights. Hence, the provision of human rights is automatically linked with the concept of social justice.

Part - III

Rousseau on Justice in General Will

The Status of Justice in early enlightenment is based on the social contract of Hobbes, Locke, and Rousseau. The social contract theory of the state implies that there was a time when men lived without any recognised civil law or without the state. The idea of the social contract is one of the foundations of the just society and because it emphasise on equality of all human being to enter into agreement to create a just society. It is the belief that the just state only exists to serve the will of the people, and they are the source of all political power enjoyed by the state. In Rousseau's general will underlies the vision of justice.

Jean-Jacques Rousseau was one of the most influential thinkers during the enlightenment period in eighteenth century in Europe. His conception of general will and its vision of justice are also based on the theory of the social contract. Rousseau advocates a social contract which is based on general will through which a proper and just society by common agreement can be formed. General will is the true will of each of state's members in which each individual gives up his right to control his life in exchange for an equal voice in setting the ground rules of a society. He appeals to the people to surrender their private will to a new moral and collective body with one will which he calls the general will of the society. Rousseau believes that general will is the procedural components in formulating the notion of justice. His notion of justice is regulated in the principle of general will. He emphasised on the principle of generality or common interest in shaping the laws of any political and social institution. The just laws are those that reflect a political community's general will or common good.

Before exploring further relationship between general will and justice, it will be imperative to explain the notion of social contract in Rousseau. In his highly acclaimed book, *TheSocial Contract*, Rousseau discusses his notion of general will in terms of social contract. Rousseau begins about social contract with the observation that "man is born free and everywhere he is in chains. One believes himself the master of others, and yet he is a greater slave than they are"[32]. Rousseau observes that though man is born free but still they are in social and political relations with other beings. In Rousseau's social contract, everyone is free as everyone forfeits the same amount of rights and imposes the same duties on all. He argued that since the participants in the social and political process must be free, it.is illogical for a man to surrender his freedom for slavery. Further, he argued that even if one thinks of himself to be master but still he's slave to others in terms of social and political obligations. No one can be a master of others because the slave and master relationship will ever-changing process. At a time one can be a slave and the other can be master and vice versa. The social contract and its act of association consist of a reciprocal commitment between society and the individual. Each individual in making a contract finds himself committed in two ways; first as a member of the sovereign body in relation to individuals, and secondly as a member of the state in relation to the sovereign.

According to Rousseau's theory of social contract, people voluntarily transfer their personal rights to the civil society or community in return for security of life and property. "The passing from the state of nature to civil society produces a remarkable change in man; it puts rationality and justice as rule of conduct in the place of instincts and gives his action the moral quality the previously lacked in the state of nature"[33]. In the state of nature there comes a time when individuals can no longer maintain themselves in traditional independence, and becomes necessary for self-preservation to unite to form a society. He argues that people should form a society to which they would completely surrender themselves. By giving up their rights, they actually create a new entity in the form of a public person that would be directed by a general will. When people join the community, they willingly agree to comply with the general will of the community. According to Rousseau,

> The social contract discover a form of association which will defend and protect with the whole common force the person and goods of each associate and while uniting himself with all, may still obey himself alone and remain as before. This the fundamental problem of which the social contract provides the solution[34].

His theory of social contract is based on an analysis of the contractual social and political relationships that may be necessary for a legitimate government, and it is an explanation of how these relationships may combine the principles of justice.

Rousseau maintains that civil society is based on a contractual arrangement or order of rights and duties which applies equally to all people. In contractual arrangement, natural liberty is exchanged for civil liberty and whereby natural rights are exchanged for legal rights. The terms and conditions of the contract provide assurance that civil laws promote the public good rather than the private good of particular individual and group. He says, "The strongest man is never strong enough to be master all the time, unless the transforms force into right and obedience into duty"[35]. For him, justice cannot be defined in terms of the power of some powerful individuals to gain advantage over others. If justice were the same as the power to gain advantage over others then the most powerful individuals would always be the most just and morally right. Justice can only prevail when the powerful and strongest of men transform the force of power into obligation and duty. So the justice consists in not treating others as an unequal or slave but equal to all. Moreover, if justice were the power to force an individual to adhere to a particular demand then there would be no obligation for an individual to comply with a lawful authority unless that authority had the power to force the individual to comply. Thus, justice can be achieved in society when individuals and civil authority can act in harmony with, and fulfil their moral obligations toward each other. It may not depend on whether individuals can be forced to comply with civil authority. Moreover, there may be a moral obligation to comply with civil authority if that authority is legitimate. Then the authority must be based on a fair and just agreement among the members of society, the society will establish well organized and just society.

The transition from the state of nature to the civil society is to bring about justice. This passing from the state of nature to the civil society produces a remarkable change in the member of community; because it enhances equality, peace, harmony and justice. The society must develop from a social contract in which every individual voluntarily participate in making laws. Rousseau, like Hobbes postulate a single contract and thereby creates absolute, indivisible sovereignty. Sovereignty according to Rousseau, is not vested in a ruler apart from society itself as Hobbes has assumed, instead it is vested in the people themselves. According to Rousseau, "as nature gives each man an absolute power over all his members, the social compact gives the body politic an absolute power over all of its (members); and it is this very power which, directed by the general will, has the name sovereignty"[36]. Each man is sovereign to unite into a general will and this sovereignty of will make laws.

When people enter into the social contract, they surrender their individual rights to their collective whole. Rousseau argues.

> The political community must have a convention as its basis, for only such a convention, could produce a respectable reason for the obedience of men in society. The social contract, which defines this convention, consists of total surrender of all rights by all citizens to the body politic as a whole; this surrender produces a sovereign, composed all members of the society and alone capable of enacting the rules by which men will live together. These rules or acts of sovereignty are only legitimate when they proceed from

the general which is the enlightened self-interest of each member of the entire community when directed to the problem of the community. The generality of law provides a criterion for legitimacy on the assumption that man freely wills his action and cannot by his very natures, will to do himself harm or injustice[37].

Rousseau regards convention as the basis for the obedience of its members in the society. The convention demands that once individuals enter into the social agreement they surrender their individual interest to the good of the whole. Each citizen has the natural liberty of independent life for the civil society protected by the state allowing social rights. For Rousseau, It must take place in a way that also secures the unity of all in a desire for what will most benefit the whole. This is the fundamental purpose of all social and political institutions to secure the participation of every individual in the general will.

Rousseau's concept of general will in the social contract is not merely the sum of all the individual wills who participate but the will of all. When the individuals enter into the agreement to seek the welfare of the community and consensus regarding the welfare of all, the general will must be concerned solely with the general interest, which is the inalienable responsibility of the sovereign body expressed through legislation.

Rousseau's aim in the social contract is to demonstrate the possibility of legitimate political authority and obligation. In political society there can be legitimate and sure principle of government. In the social contract, Rousseau is dealing in the hypothetical mood with abstract problem which seems to him to emerge from philosophical reflection on the actual nature of man and the possible order of laws and government. On Rousseau's view, "The social contract is a genuine and legitimate contract, which is to the benefit of everyone, since it unites liberty with law and utility with right"[38]. The social contract approach is beneficial to all the members of the society or the state. It is a genuine and legitimate contract as it unites liberty with law and utility with right. "The state of *The Social Contract* is a community united by the general will and the sense of a community on the part of its citizen is necessary for the maintenance and well-being of all"[39].

In the social contract the general will is the moral sovereignty to give impartial laws for all.

Rousseau contends that,

> Sovereignty is nothing but the exercise of the general will or that a state is established when individuals place themselves under the supreme direction of the general will. In social pact, each one of us puts into the community his person and all his powers under the supreme direction of the general will and as a body, then we incorporate every member as an indivisible part of the whole[40].

The social contract states that each of us puts his person and his power in common interest under general will and each member as an indivisible part of the whole. This kind of association creates a moral and collective body which we called the state. The will or the general will of the sovereign is always right and each citizen share and participate in the general will.As RadcliffBenjamin says,

> Rousseau begins with the notion that all individuals are autonomous agents who share an absolute natural equality. Men are born free, bound to no one but themselves enjoying unlimited liberty. The state of nature are not the state of 'war of all against all' proposed by Hobbes, is neither dangerous nor uncomfortable. Rational agents come to see that to survive and to flourish they must invent cost-sharing mechanisms so as to provide themselves with the public goods of peace and security[41].

In essence, this requires the establishment of civil society that enhances justice. To create a society is to establish the relationships necessary to provide collective will needs some form of contract among individuals whereby they agree to such. This process takes the form of agreement denoted as the social contract in which all individuals assent is necessary to formulate a new order.

Rousseau provides the notion of the general will for linking harmony with majority rule. Society, he suggests should be governed exclusively in terms of the common interests of its members. This shared interest is the public good and is always the object of the general will. Thus what the people wish as a corporate entity is their collective interest, that is, the general will, as opposed to merely the sum of their individual interests, private will. "The Social Contract contrasts general wills with private or particular will. A general will is said to be the will of 'the whole community', the private will are ascribed paradigmatically to individuals in a state of nature"[42]. The just state exists only when laws are made by individuals expressing their views rather than the opinion of private will as given by their preferences. In this way, the general will is the true will of all citizens. Accordingly, if law is a product of the general will then all individuals must by definition assent to it. Laws predicated upon the general will are thus agreed to by all individuals and are thus legitimate, just and for the betterment of all. Thus, the social contract is a detailed set of procedural rules for making further substantive rules, which are sovereign expressions of the general will. The general will become the source of political and social justice because it is based on social contract. This conception of law ensures equal justice to all. That's why he proposes that law comes before justice because the sense of justice comes out from law of particular institutions.

General will in the social contract plays a very important role in formulating the concept of justice in Rousseau's thought. Rousseau's status of justice is derived from his description of the general will in the social contract. His sense of justice consists in the principle of generality, commonality, impartiality, universality, equality of all citizens. Rousseau's conviction is that justice consists of strict generality and impartiality. As we have seen, the status of justice in the general will is perfectly general with respect to any given political community. It is based on general both in the sense that it reflects the general welfare of the whole community, and it is general with respect to each member who has contributed to making just society. Justice in the general will implies that the just and proper rules with respect to all members of the social and political community.

Thus, the concept of general will is the backbone of the modern procedural view of justice in Rousseau. The principle of generality helps to formulate the laws of any given political community and social institutions. For Rousseau, laws and justice are complementary to each other. Laws of any institutions provide the basis for making the just society. However, there are some distinct and identifiable dimensions to Rousseau's conception of justice. Firstly, the notion of justice is based on the principle of generality which refers to the general interest of the people. Justice relates to commonality, or the public good of the entire community. As Rousseau says,

> General laws take into account the well-being of the whole political community and not just its largest or most influential parts. Laws cannot be truly general if they omit the concerns of any significant element of the political community. Conversely, partial laws that privilege the interests of one group at the expense of another or the community as a whole are defective insofar as they fail to achieve the generality that follows from aggregating what Rousseau calls the sums of the differences[43].

Justice consists of applying general rules impartially to all men regardless of their circumstances and differences.

Secondly, in order for laws and principles of justice to be considered truly just and perfect, they must be impartial in the sense that they do not concern for particular persons or groups. For Rousseau, justice in generality requires laws to be abstract and indifferent to the particular identities of the persons. Rousseau's citizens legislate by means of rules that are abstract and impersonal, indifferent to private identities or differences among the citizens. The more appropriate meaning of generality is universality. As Rousseau writes, "When I say that the object of the laws is always general, I mean that the law considers the subjects in a body and their actions in the abstract, never any man as an individual or a particular action"[44]. Justice can prevail when man acts in the state against his self-interest will under the direction of the general will. The individual in this kind of situation is does not lose his personal freedom. In fact, the constraint of the general will is instrumental for securing of his ultimate freedom which reconciles freedom of each with freedom of all. The concept of general will is the heart of Rousseau's perspective on justice, which must be distinguished from other types of human will. Rousseau's concept of general will is always right, that it, it is the will that when one thinks of the justice toward entire humanity and the common good as well and not of one's own particular will as a private person. The sense of justice will come only when every individual's will is motivated by his ultimate and collective interest for the progress of the society.

Third, justice and laws not only have to be formally general and articulated in terms of universal rules; they also and maybe more importantly presuppose an intrinsic moral equality among citizens. To prove his point, Rousseau says, "Thus by the nature of the pact...every genuine act of the general will either obligates or favours all citizens equally, so that the Sovereign knows only the body of the nation and does not single out any one of those who make it up"[45]. As Rousseau postulates a single contract and creates absolute sovereignty and for him laws consists in absolute sovereignty which is not vested in the king or government apart from the society itself. Instead, it is vested in the people themselves. Sovereignty lies in the will of citizens themselves. The nature of social contract based on general will obligates and favours all citizens equally.

Fourth, it is not enough for justice and laws to reflect the general interest or well-being of the whole community; they must also be products of the community actively exercising its collective will. According to Rousseau, "Not only must the subject matter with regard to which the statute is being enacted" be general, but so too must be the enacting will"[46]. Here generality implies that laws are not imposed from the outside upon a passive people, but arise actively from the body of the people themselves. Their legitimacy derives from the fact that they are generally assented to, by the people as a whole.

Lastly, the final test of a just law is whether it is reasonable and just for an entire political community including for ourselves. One has to understand, Rousseau notes, "that what generalizes the will is not so much the number of voices as it is the common interest which unites them: for the general will is an assented will in which everyone necessarily submits to the same conditions which he imposes on others"[47]. General will demands that in a given situation what one expects from others must also impose on oneself the same set of rules. Due to this harmony of interest, justice gives to social deliberation of equality. "Given the equality that structures the terms of their association within the social contract, no citizen has the right to require another to do what he himself does not do[48]. If we are unwilling to submit ourselves to a law, then it is illegitimate for us to impose it on our fellow citizens, and vice-versa. Justice is the product of a kind of reciprocity informed by reason as much as by the will.

Rousseau's notion of justice in general will is also based on the social pact which establishes equality among the citizens in that they all pledge themselves under the same conditions and must all enjoy the same rights. Hence by nature of contract everyone's act of sovereignty or the every act of the general will binds all the citizens equally, so the sovereign recognise the whole body of the nation and makes no distinction and discrimination between any of the members who compose it.

Rousseau's view of justice lies in general will and its basis is the social contract, equitable one, common to all, it can have no end but the common good. Status of justice is general with respect to the whole political community and social institution. It is impartiality and universality in the sense general as opposed to merely partial or interested. It is also equality and uniformity of applying generally to all members of the political community equally and in precisely the same way irrespective of their differences.

To bring this chapter to an end, I can conclude early enlightenment thinkers especially Locke repudiated innate ideas in formulating his theory of epistemology. Locke's conception of justice begins with the criticism of the Descartes's innate ideas or a priori ideas and replaces it by sensation and a posteriori ideas in epistemology. Epistemology is one of the important tools to know about the principle of justice. It helps us that how to make our society just by using experience and freedom rather than reason only. It is the epistemology which gives the idea of social contract, toleration, human right, and fraternity and justice as well.

The concept of justice begins with the overthrow of the monarch's special rights and replaces it by the natural rights of human beings. The status of justice in enlightenment, I think culminateshistorically in the political disorder of the French Revolution. The French Revolution brought an end to the monarchical or traditional hierarchical political and social order, the political power and authority of the Catholic Church were violently destroyed and replaced by the liberal ideals of freedom, autonomy, rights, toleration and equality for all.

At the time of pre enlightenment, the conception of justice did not exist because the sovereign power concentrated in the hands of monarchic system. The monarch was able to declare law, issue commands and take political decisions such as determining public goals and their priorities which were binding all individuals and kept it within his jurisdiction. The monarch issues laws according to his own will rather than individual's consent to formulate laws and order. However, enlightenment thinkers brought about a very powerful approach on the scene and that was the social contract approach. This was inspired by the background of monarch system where all opportunities were distributed unequally or unjustly.

Early enlightenment thinkers such as Locke and Rousseau have tried to establish a just or equal society through the method of social contract to maintain individual rights, equality, toleration, and general will. The status of justice in liberalism represents a synthesis of the principle of autonomy, individualism, equality, liberty, toleration, generality and universality. They have analysed their principle of justice which deals with greater autonomy, liberty, human rights, toleration and fraternity. For liberalists, justice is a thread which runs throughout these values and make them parts of the integrated whole of the just society.

It was the early enlightenment that provides the sense of justice from the social contract tradition which presents the new version of the origin of the society which governed and controlled through constitution which is divided into three parts namely, legislative, judiciary and executive. For Locke maintaining justice legislative and executive must be separated. That's why he emphasised that to evolve a just state, enlightened being's representative makes the just principles and the state should apply them to deliver equal and impartial justice. That's why liberalists believed that constitution has been created with a definite purpose to serve certain social needs and to deliver justice. Locke's and Rousseau's social contract establishes just society or legitimate society that obtains legitimacy from the consent of those who willingly consent to make law and order to enhance justice, peace harmony.

Notes

1. Locke,*An Essay Concerning Human Understanding*. p. 16.
2. *Ibid.,* pp. 16-17.
3. *Ibid.,* p. 42-43.
4. *Ibid.,* p. 43.
5. Singh.*Kant and Hegel Methodology, Ontology, Epistemologyand Dialectic*. p. 120.
6. Locke. *An Essay Concerning Human Understanding*. pp. 271-72.
7. Singh, *Freedom and Causation with Special Reference to Hegel's Overcoming of Kant*. p. 23.
8. *Ibid.,* pp. 23-24.
9. Locke, *Two Treatise of Government*, pp. 330-31.
10. Locke. *First Treatise on Civil Government*, p. 28.
11. Locke. *Two Treatise of Government*, p. 267.
12. *Ibid.,* p. 269.
13. Ruth, W. Grant. "Locke's Political Anthropology and Lockean Individualism," pp. 42-63.
14. Locke, *First Treatise on Civil Government,* p. 30.
15. *Ibid,* p. 94.
16. Locke. *Two Treatise of Government*, pp. 94-95.
17. Harris, A. Edward. "From Social Contract to Hypothetical Agreement: Consent and the Obligation to Obey the Law", p. 651.
18. *Ibid.*, p. 652.
19. Edman Irwin, *The Works of Plato*, p. 102.
20. *Hobbes, Leviathan*. p. 45.
21. Locke, *The Second Treatise of Government*. p.4.
22. *Ibid.,* p. 73.
23. Locke, *The Second Treatise of Government*. p. 32.
24. Locke,*Two Treatise of Government*. p. 95.
25. *Ibid.,* p. 5.
26. *Ibid.,* p. 15.
27. *Ibid.,* p. 16.
28. Locke, *The Second Treatise of Government*. p. 54-55.
29. Edward, A. Harris. "*From Social Contract to Hypothetical Agreement: Consent and the Obligation to Obey,"* p. 651.

30. Monique, Deveaux, "Toleration and Respect," pp. 407-427.
31. Locke. *A Latter Concerning Toleration*, p. 631.
32. Rousseau. *The Social Contract*. p. 49.
33. *Ibid.,* p. 64.
34. Rousseau. *The Social Contract*. p. 49.
35. *Ibid.,* p. 49.
36. Roger D. Mater, *Political philosophy of Rousseau*. p. 318.
37. *Ibid.,* pp. 349-50.
38. Rousseau. *The Social Contract*. pp. 27-28.
39. Andrew, Levine, *The General Will: Rousseau, Marx, communism*, p. 40.
40. *Ibid.,* p. 61.
41. Benjamin, Radcliff. "The General Will and Social Choice Theory Source," pp. 34-35.
42. Andrew, Levine. *The General Will: Rousseau, Marx, communism*, p. 18.
43. Rousseau, *The Social Contract*. p. 72.
44. *Ibid.,* p. 80.
45. *Ibid.,* p. 74.
46. *Ibid.,* p. 81-82
47. *Ibid.,* p.76.
48. *Ibid.,* 144.

Chapter - 2

Kant on Enlightenment Rationality and Morality

In this chapter I will examine and explicate Kant's position on enlightenment rationality and morality. In the enlightenment rationality Kant has tried to overcome the logical inconsistencies which we find in Locke and Rousseau. Kant has developed individuals to the level of autonomy and sovereignty and in order to substantiate these doctrines he has advocated categorical imperatives. The categorical imperative is the most fundamental principle of morality that can be derived from the good will. Kant argued that we must have free will to follow thc principlc of catcgorical impcrativc.

The Enlightenment rationality is an intellectual movement of reform that swept the monarchy system of special rights throughout Europe and North America during the 18th century. Enlightenment rationality brought a great change in the society such as freedom equality, fraternity and justice by emphasising on equal freedom, rights, tolerance, and autonomy, public and private reason to every human being as a rational being. It is "emergence from man's self-incurred immaturity to maturity"[1]. It is focused on freedom to use one's own understanding to become an enlightened being. In fact, it inculcates the habit of moving from immaturity to understanding to exercise right, autonomy, tolerance and public as well as private reason to reach the stage of enlightenment. It is the enlightenment which focuses on individuals to become autonomous to use their right which automatically creates the habit of tolerance, which leads reciprocal attitude toward others right, autonomy, freedom of public and private reason to create equality, peace and justice in the society.

It is the enlightenment and morality which awakens individuals to become autonomous to formulate self-imposed laws of morality. The sense of autonomy requires so that individuals construct self-imposed by which they act. These self-imposed laws must be compatible with categorical imperative so that it can be harmonise with the maxims of other enlightened being. It is the categorical imperative which evaluates individual's maxims either they are just or unjust through rational comprehension of the universal law. Morality treats every individual equally that is according to general principle or rule and this rule that binds all rational beings into one law is called categorical imperative which determine which maxims ought to be for the decisions of our will. Kant's principle of categorical imperative must be necessary universal and sufficient to determine actions. It provides a vision of moral and just society wherein every man gets universal and equal treatment in terms of freedom and right for social and political action to become the enlightened and moral man as well.

For the sake of clarity and precision, I shall divide the present chapter into the fallowing two parts.

Part I, Kant on right, tolerance, autonomy, public and private reason.

Part II, Kant on Free-will, Categorical Imperative, Good will.

Before coming to the basic issues which I shall be dealing in the above two parts, I would like to point out that Kant with respect to his enlightenment rationality and morality is based on the very notion of freedom. I want to claim that enlightenment rationality and morality in the context of freedom is an important concern for the image of just and moral man. I propose to explain this claim through an understanding of Immanuel Kant's essay on enlightenment. As I have already stated that freedom is the most operative term in Kant's enlightenment and morality, it states that freedom is to use one's own understanding without the guidance of other. However, Kant's enlightenment and freedom, especially freedom to use of public reason is the main concern to reach at the stage of enlightenment in one aspect. The other aspect is the morality which makes a sense if the action is guided with freedom and rationality. In enlightenment and morality, he conceives of freedom in terms of independence than in terms of non-interference. The power of independence and thereby overcoming immaturity is the most important slogan of enlightenment. With this brief remark regarding freedom is the most operative term in Kant's enlightenment and morality; I shall come to the Part I of the chapter.

Part - I

Kant on rights, tolerance, autonomy, public and private reason

The stage of enlightenment was the beginning of a just society where enlightenment thinkers repudiated monarch's privileges and brought out the question of individual rights in the society. Enlightenment is one is one of the most debated themes of contemporary intellectual discourse. The eighteenth century claims that progress is possible only through the use of reason. During this time there is remarkable great changes occurred in scientific thought and invention. New ideas filled the horizon and man was eager to explore these ideas freely. Man began to embrace an exaggerated belief in the perfection of humanity based on reason, clear thinking. They severely criticized the medieval extremism of mysticism and superstitions and changed their opinion to the other extremes of reason and rationality. It also brought about a great change in the society because at that time reason, rationality, freedom, equality, justice became the central part of human affairs. The age of enlightenment provided the stage where people were free to pursue individual rights, liberty, equality and justice.

Kant begins his discussion on enlightenment in the famous essay, *An Answer to the Question: What is Enlightenment?* The spread of enlightenment and knowledge is summed up in Kant's dictum "Have courage to use your own reason"[2]. Kant insisted on the use of reason for understanding. He says that we should have courage to use our own reason. The enlightenment rationality is the ultimate outcome of just man by giving right, tolerance, autonomy, equality, fraternity, justice, public and private reason. It focuses that human beings are free to make and transform their institutions in accordance with their own critical rationality. Reason alone can enlighten humanity from the biasness of tradition, custom, and inherited authority and allow them to realize freedom by submitting their own conscious purposes. Here, we can say that "*sapereaude*or have courage to use your own understanding to become just man"[3]. Enlightenment traditions of rights, freedom, tolerance, autonomy, public and private use of reason are the pre-requisite for the image of just man within the society. Once the individual moves from ignorance to enlightenment he or she can become a just by overcoming his immaturity, irrationality.

In Kant's *Critique of Judgment*, the phrase he had employed as the motto and dream of enlightenment which serves as the first of his three maxims of understanding: first, "think for oneself; second, think from the standpoint of everyone else; and third, think always consistently. The first is the maxim of an unprejudiced, the second of a broadened, and the third of a consistent way of thinking"[4]. Further, Kant says that "it is only by becoming skilled at the first two which he labelled the maxims of understanding and of judgment- that we become proficient in the third, which he called the maxim of reason"[5]. We become enlightened and reasonable thinking for ourselves, by thinking from the standpoint of everyone else, and thinking consistently.

Kant elaborated the concept of enlightenment in his article on "*An Answer to the Question: What is Enlightenment*?" Kant says,

> Enlightenment is man's emergence from his self-incurred immaturity. Immaturity is the ability to use one's own understanding without the guidance of another. This immaturity is self-imposed, because reason itself languishes not in lack of understanding but only of resolve and courage to solve oneself without direction from another. *Sapereaude*; Think boldly, take courage, and use your own understanding to serve: This is therefore the motto of the Enlightenments[6].

When a human being reaches to eenlightenment stage then human beings departs from his self-incurred habits and is able to use one's own reason without the guidance of another. The immaturity emerged not from a lack of reason but from the lack of courage to use one's reason and understanding without the guidance of another. In other words, it is the point at which a human being recognizes his or her own autonomy and rights. It develops reason to the extent that it becomes autonomous and gets rid of restraints from tradition and authority. "The way to enlightenment Kant emphasizes is not to seek a mentor or authority in thinking, in willing and in feeling"[7]. He has placed freedom and maturity at the centre of enlightenment. In enlightenment, freedom plays an important role because freedom makes public use of one's own reason in all matters.

Kant has placed the freedom and maturity at the centre of enlightenment and contrasted it from tutelages. "Tutelage meant man's inability to make use of his understanding without direction from another for instance, self-incurred is this tutelage when its cause lies not in lack of reason but in lack of resolution and courage to use it without direction from another"[8]. It has been often been pointed out that this emergence from tutelage and so called immaturity is a social matter for Kant. Kant claims that

> It is difficult for an individual to free himself from minority by the cultivation of his own spirit. Despite the difficulty facing individual attempts to achieve enlightenment however, it is possible for a public to enlighten itself. This enlightenment of the public is almost inevitable if only the public is left in freedom[9].

On Kant's view, public use of reason must always be free and it alone can bring about enlightenment among men, while private use of reason can be restricted. As enlightenment is the emergence of maturity and freedom to use public use of reason from immaturity and irrational behaviour guided by others in the form of authority, tradition and customs.

After discussing Kant's essay on enlightenment, there is need to explore Kant's perspective of freedom, universal right, tolerance, autonomy, public and private reason to know the characteristic of humanity. Kant focuses on the principle of freedom and autonomy of the will, that is, the important ingredient in transforming the characteristic of just and enlightened man. On Kant's view, freedom and the autonomy of the will is the prerequisite to become enlightened and just individual. It is the enlightenment rationality which brings out the individual rights, tolerance, autonomy and other human-centric concepts. When Kant faced the question that whether we are enlightened or not; Kant responded, "When the question is asked do we live in an enlightened epoch then the answer is: No but rather in an epoch of enlightenment. Here the question arise do we now live in an *enlightened age?* The answer could be no, but we do live in an *age of enlightenment*"[10]. The age which we live in is not enlightened age but we live in the age of enlightenment where we all have the potential to become enlightened. As matters now stand, much is still lacking for men to be completely able or even to be placed in a situation where they would be able to use their own reason confidently and properly in religious and political matters without the guidance of another. Yet we have clear indications that the field is now being opened for them to work freely toward enlightenment.

For this enlightenment, however, nothing is required but freedom. It is the freedom to make public use of one's reason at every point. Now the question arises what kind of freedom becomes barrier in the way of enlightenment? It is the restriction of freedom to use public reason becomes obstacle in enlightenment. As Kant says in his article:- *An Answer to the Question of What is Enlightenment*,

> I hear on all sides, 'Do not argue'! The Officer says: 'Do not argue but drill!' The tax collector: 'Do not argue but pay!' The cleric: 'Do not argue but believe!' Only one ruler in the world says, 'Argue as much as you will, and about what you will, but obey!' So, everywhere there is restriction on freedom. Which restriction is an obstacle to enlightenment, and which is not an obstacle but a promoter of it? I answer: The public use of one's reason must always be free, and it alone can bring about enlightenment among men. The private use of reason, on the other hand, may often be very narrowly restricted without particularly hindering the progress of enlightenment. By the public use of one's reason I understand the use, which a person makes of it as a scholar before the reading public. Private use I call that which one may make of it in a particular civil post or office, which is entrusted[11].

It is the enlightenment rationality which gives the freedom to use an understanding to become an enlightened man. As it encourages individual to move from ignorance to reason and to implement right, autonomy, tolerance and public as well as private reason to reach the stage of enlightened age rather than age of enlightenment.

Having discussed Kant's position on enlightenment, now I will discuss how enlightenment ingredient such as human right, tolerance, autonomy and public and private reason that helps to transform in the age of enlightenment to the enlightened age where every rational man acquires the characteristics of a just man so that everyone live in an *enlightened epoch* rather in an *epoch of enlightenment* which was the motto and dream of Kant.

Behind the notion of rights, autonomy, tolerance, public and private reason, there is a deeper philosophy and that is the philosophy of European enlightenment. As we know that there have been a certain attempts to define rights in terms of the constitution of nation, ethnic and religious identities, etc. To define rights in the most general sense, Kant's categorical imperative is one of the principles that could be taken into account. The maxims of categorical imperative cannot be strange to any culture though they could implement to every culture because they are universal. One can easily imagine that the absence of any maxim could be tantamount to the denial of the human dignity. Therefore maxims could be regarded as the necessary principles for any study of human right. Now the basic question arises- what is a right and what is the right of humanity? Kant sometimes speaks of the right of humanity as the liberty of each "to seek his happiness in whatever way seems best to him"[12]. Every individual should lead as an autonomous life and free to pursue their one's own end.

However, Jonathan Peterson says in his article, "Enlightenment and Freedom," "right of humanity is not defined as a right to the pursuit of happiness, but as a right not to be subject to the will of others".[13] Kantian notion of freedom implies in the act of independence from constrained by other's choices of individuals. Kant says in his *Science of Right,*

> The only original right, belonging to each man in virtue of his humanity is freedom.... And there is only one innate right, the

> birth right of freedom. Freedom is independence of the compulsory will of another; and in so far as it can coexist with the freedom of all according to a universal law, it is the one sole original, inborn right belonging to every man in virtue of his humanity. There is, indeed, an innate equality belonging to every man which consists in his right to be independent of being bound by others to anything more than that to which he may also reciprocally bind them"[14]

Every individual has natural right i.e. right to freedom which ought not to be constrained by other human being. Each and every man is equal in terms of rights and the master of one's own right as a rational being. "Freedom which is independence from being constrained by another's choice insofar as it can coexist with the freedom of every other in accordance with a universal law"[15]. We can infer from the above statement that when Kant develops freedom as the only original right of man, and he proposes to limit that freedom in the case of each individual solely by the demand for an equal freedom on the part of all otherindividuals. Freedom is the only original right belonging to every individual by virtue of his humanity. It is independence of the heteronomy of the will of another and it can coexist with the freedom of all according to a universal law, that is, categorical imperative.

Kant says about universal principle of right by saying that, "Every action is right which in itself, or in the maxim, on which it proceeds, is such that it can coexist along with the freedom of the will of each and all in action, according to a universal law"[16]. It means that, if one's free action generally can coexist with the freedom of others in according to a universal law. For instance, any one does me a wrong and who curtails hinders me in the performance of this action. Then such hindrance and obstruction in terms of wrong behaviour with me cannot coexist accordance with the freedom of universal laws. It is evidently clear that for Kant an action would be contrary to right if it interferes with the formal freedom of one's neighbour.

It may be, however, pointed out that Kant makes a distinction between private and public right. "The right of freedom in terms of independence leads first to private right, which governs the interaction of free persons, and then to public right, which requires the creation of constitutional state"[17]. Independence is the basic principle of right. It guarantees equal freedom, and it requires that no person should be subject to the will of another. The core idea of independence in enlightenment rationality is an articulation of the distinction between persons and things. A person is a being capable of setting his or her own purposes, while a thing is something that can be used in pursuit of purposes. Once the person becomes autonomous, he or she gets right which automatically creates the habit of tolerance. Tolerance is right centric. Basically, it is a permissive and reciprocal attitude toward others right, autonomy, freedom of public and private reason etc. It is our duty to respect others who have different opinions, religious belief, race and practices than your own. It is the enlightenment which emphasise on the fundamental concept of tolerance which create peace and justice in the society. It tried to give the image of just man by inculcating the habit of tolerance to live peacefully by accepting others dignity, right and autonomy. It promotes the habit to live to get along and learning to get along. It is one of the important duties to allow others to have the same right to their beliefs, opinions, race, caste, creed, and sexuality and others differences among individuals.

Enlightenment rationality, therefore, focus that each and every individual ought to be tolerant and accepting others differences and once we have acquire this habit automatically lead to a more peaceful and just world for all of us. The contemporary commentator on Kant, Onora O'Neill writes in book, *Constructions of Reason,*

> Toleration in the Kantian picture is then not only merely a political virtue or practice that would have to be a part of any achieved just polity or society. It is the only matrix within which a plurality of potentially reasoning beings can constitute the full authority of reason and so become able to debate without restrictions what a just political constitution might be[18].

Tolerance has the potential to debate without any restriction and reach to consensus through reasoning in formulating any political constitution. It shows that toleration unites and binds all human being into a just society where all human being can express themselves properly. Kant's concept of tolerance is a duty to respect others right.

It is embedded in our culture through the enlightenment thinkers especially Kant's enlightenment rationality to make an individual become just to himself and others.

Kant's enlightenment emphasised on autonomy of individual that every individual is autonomous and can lead his life according to self-interest. However, the point here is not only that individual knows what is in their own self-interest but also that it is good for individuals to tolerate others be able to pursue their own good in their own way. This kind of approach requires autonomy is pre-requisite and important for individuals to know their own good and the most important is that there should be a distinction between self-regarding action and actions that affects others right. In this way the principle of tolerance bring the habit of enlightened being to pursue own interest and gives opportunity to others so that that they also become enlightened. However, the sense of toleration should be practiced only in the context of freedom to public use of reason. For Kant, "the importance of toleration is connected with the very grounding of reason, and so in particular with the very grounding of practical reason"[19]. For Kant, public use of reason must always be free and toleration of public use of reason is necessary for the emergence of the generally shared standards of reasoning that fully supports public enlightenment. If we undermine the public use of reason by intolerance, Kant's enlightenment would not be achieved.

The enlightenment of Kant gives the images of just man by inculcating the habit of tolerance of others right in order to find the best way to livein terms of self-interest and others interest. Therefore, it makes individual to be a just by tolerating and giving respect to others right and freedom so that everyone irrespective of cast, creed, sex, and religion coexist and live peacefully and just fully. I can say that only enlightened person can tolerate and willingly accept the principle and criteria of general binding norms in a pluralist global society.

The conception of toleration leads to the recognition of others autonomous existence. The most important contribution in formulating the notion of autonomy is Kant. The concept of autonomy in Kant's philosophy plays a central role. The concept of autonomy has been one of the essential human concept play an important role in Kant's enlightenment rationality. Kant's enlightenment emphasised on autonomy of individual that every individual is autonomous and can lead his life according to his own rational interest. In enlightened age, rationality and freedom are regarded as one of the compulsory condition for the exercise of right and personal autonomy. The quest for autonomy has been a pervasive ideal in the twentieth-century of enlightenment and moral philosophy and most of the philosophers have defended some version of autonomy. As Robert Noggle writes,

> Freedom and autonomy are necessary for an individual to be a just man. Only rational beings can be subject to the moral law and come out from immaturity to maturity. Respecting individuals means respecting individual's rationality, freedom and right. We must respect person because of their rationality[20].

Autonomy is one of the important foundations of enlightenment the only autonomous being can use their own understanding to come out form immaturity to maturity and become enlightened person.

Kant had presumed, in his *Groundwork of theMetaphysic of Morals*, "the literal meaning of autonomy is obedience to a self-imposed law"[21]. He treated it as a constraint, a rule of moral conduct that is objective in the sense that it is what all rational beings would agree ought to be done. It reveals a shift of attention from the constraining force of the rules chosen by autonomous agents to the character of those agents and the process by which they reach decisions. Kant says in *Critique of Practical Reason,* "Reason determines the will in a practical law that directly, not through an intervening feeling of pleasure or displeasure, even if this pleasure is taken in the law itself"[22]. It is clear that Kant's autonomy is always guided through rational human will. Rationality is an autonomous source of individual's action. It is the property of rational being. Autonomy of human being is the property of it by which it is a law to itself independently of any property of objects of volition. Autonomy is the foundation of enlightenment to become just. It is the autonomy that helps an individual to get rid of tradition and superstition and lead an authentic life. It helps men to come out from ignorance to reach in the age of enlightened where autonomy guides how to use understanding. It gives men the capacity to engage in a continuing process of criticism and re-evaluation in men. It provides the higher order capacity to choose his or her ends. The main requirement of enlightened and just man is that the choices be truly one's own that one must not have been manipulated, brainwashed or conditioned into making them.

Now in enlightenment rationality, the idea of autonomy plays an important role and it requires that the rational being has courage to think boldly and has sense of right and wrong in any decision making. For Kant, it is the duty of every one to have courage to use their reason, freedom, right and toleration under the self-legislative moral law so that it becomes universal.

In Kant's enlightenment project, everyone can reach to the enlightened stage, if they can become autonomous and subjects one's will to self-imposed maxim like *courage to use own understanding.* For Kant, enlightenment requires autonomy that individuals make themselves the law by which they act. That law, of course, must be the *categorical imperative*. Thus, autonomous individuals alone can claim an absolute right to be treated according to the moral law (as ends rather than as means only) because they are capable of self-legislation and are not simply as a puppets. Dream of Kant's enlightened age ought to achieve if every man acquire the characteristic of autonomy so that everyone can act as a free and autonomous being. They can free to feel, imagine, speculate and construct their own meaning. They have their own evolving vision and are free to discover themselves. Hopefully, the concept of autonomy provides an alternative perspective on the most vital question of how to choose one's mode of living to become just towards himself as well as society.

Enlightenment leads an individual to become autonomous and independence in public and private reason which automatically helps to acquire the image of just man. The debate between freedom to use public and private reason marked a turning point in the Kant's enlightenment rationality. Now it's necessary to discuss the distinction between public and private reason and what kind of freedom or autonomy promotes enlightenment. For, Kant the private use of reason is the use of reason in the context of a civil or official role. "What I call the private use of reason is that which one may make of it in a certain civil post or office with which he is entrusted"[23]. Private use of reason is required when there is need to take a decision regarding official matters. We can take examples for instance; the roles in which one can implement the private use of reason are army officer, and citizen as taxpayer and clergy man etc. In the case of the citizen as taxpayer and army officer is probably the most general example. The obedient citizen as a taxpayer has the duty to pay and obey the authority. It shows that the private use of reason is a matter of structures and relations of authority.As Kant says in his discussion of *what is enlightenment* about the "example of clergy man and citizen as a taxpayer involves acting in the name of another and carrying out another's commission"[24]. In case of private use of reason, an individual's act in accordance with the rule of authority. Although this does not preclude that someone in an official role may be required to exercise judgment in carrying out his or her tasks. It is clear that individual's use private reasons are bound to some extent. In the case of the citizens as a taxpayer, are to be bound by to pay and they will be bound by the law of authority. As a citizen, it is the moral and legal obligation to pay tax to the authority and fallow the tax rule anyhow at any cost. Therefore, private use of reason is a matter of carrying out another's commission for instance paying a tax is a matter of carrying out government's instructions. In contrast to private use of reason, the public use of one's reason deals with oneself as a freethinker. This type of reason is non- restrictiveto the individual. It is not a matter of structures and relations of authority like private use of reason. It ought to be free if the public is to become autonomous only. It builds an autonomous nature to make a self-legislative law and is to rely on their own reason without the guidance of another.

Kant's conception of public use of reason has three important features. The first, "Public reason identifies the status of those who reason publicly in terms of membership in a community. In public reason, you regard yourself as a member of a whole commonwealth, even of the society of citizens of the world."[25] The public use of reason is the use of reason of every individual as members of society where they are living. It is quite general for the betterment for humanity as a whole. The second feature is a nature of people as an audience of public reason. "Insofar as you see yourself as a member of the commonwealth of public reason, you address a public in the proper sense of the word. You speak for the betterment of public enlightenment to the public in the strict sense, that is, the world"[26]. Every enlightened person is free to use public reason to speak against government, if authority is trying to curtailed public rights of the individual. It demands that we should think for the betterment of entire humanity. The third feature emerges in Kant's discussion of the clergy example. Like the first feature, it focuses on status and on the capacities to act that go along with that status[27]. In the case of clergy, the cleric says do not argue but believe. He curtailed the freedom to clear doubt, so we cannot implement public reason in the case of clergy. However in the case of public reason, one can argue with the authority and clear the doubt. In the public use of reason, you speak in your own person. This feature of the account of public reason is particularly important, for it allows a clear distinction to be drawn between the public and private use of reason. Where the private use of reason is carried on in the name of another and involves carrying out another's commission, the public use of reason is a matter of acting on your own autonomy.

In enlightenment rationality public use of reason ought to be free and not restricted by the authority. If the public use of reason gets curtailed then individuals cannot become enlightened. It is one of the important rights of a person which helps a person to apply one's own reason for the betterment for him as well as humanity as a whole. Kant's dream of enlightenment would be unachievable. That's why it is independent from authority, unlike private use of reason that is subject to authority as well as bounded by the rules and conditions of authority. It is the moral obligation of authority to make public use of reason free so that each individual acts in one's own need and situation to evolve himself with others to become the member of Kant's enlightened age rather than age of enlightenment.

Therefore, we can say that Kant's enlightenment is an awakening call or message to human or a rational nature. It is a massage from Kant's enlightenment that each enlightened person ought to perform moral duty to bring humanity at the stage of progress. It states that one should acquire the duty of virtue to enhance oneself in terms of consciousness and other's consciousness as well with the help of public reason. In this way, we can achieve Kant's dream of enlightened age rather than age of enlightenment, if each autonomous being ought to impose a maxim such as the duty to use own understanding to make one's own progress and perfection as an end.

Part - II

Kant on Free-Will, Categorical Imperative, Good will

This section reflects on Kant's position on free will, categorical imperative, and good will. In this, I will develop how moral action ought to be implemented in terms of free will, categorical imperative and good will so that it gives the universal law that binds all human being into single principle i.e. categorical imperative. To begin with morality I will show how one's action ought to be so that it becomes universal under all circumstances.

Kant's enlightenment universalism holds that basic concepts of enlightenment such as rights, freedom, tolerance, autonomy and public and private reason should be universally applied to all rational beings. It is the enlightenment that encourages each person to become autonomous being, so that they act accordance with the universal law of morality. For instance each one should act on a maxim which can coexist with every one's action so that it becomes the universal law of morality. Kant endeavoured to create a theory of individual rights, autonomy, toleration that is universally applicable and bound others out of respect for the universal law.

The first principle of morality is that enlightenment opportunities such as freedom, liberty autonomy, toleration and freedom to use of public and private reason should be equally distributed among all individual irrespective of any differences. Kant's principle of morality and justice is meant to individual's freedom that is innate right on the basis of moral law so that it can be universalised. Kant's morality is concerned simply with principle of harmonising individual wills and their autonomy with compatible to others autonomy of will to construct the universal principle of autonomy.

Unlike utilitarian, Kantian basis of morality is freedom rather than happiness. In order to understand his conception of freedom and its implications on morality, one needs to understand how this free will becomes the central principle in the status of morality. The free will is central to Kant's theory of morality. As Kant says,

> A will is free, find the law which alone is competent to determine it necessarily. Since the material of the practical law is an object of the maxim, cannot be given except empirically, and since a free will must be independent of all empirical conditions and yet be determinable, a free will must find its ground of determination in the law, but independently of the material of the law. The legislative form is the only thing which can constitute a determining ground of the free will[28].

It states that once individuals will act according to the rational principles of categorical imperative then their act can be moral and just. In Kantian view, we can neither prove nor have certain knowledge that human beings possess free will. However, we can show that morality makes sense only if human beings are free. On the basis this assumption, we can assume that human beings are free and we can assume about the content of morality and justice in Kant's view. Kant's attempt to rationally conceive categorical imperative which shaped the universal principle of morality that all individual ought to treat equally in terms of right, autonomy and so on so. Individuals in the Kantian framework upheld others rights by contemplating the rationally intelligible universal law. Morality states that what determines our actions are ethical principles we adopt, not purposes we desire in our lives. The just principles that determine our actions are the basis of morality.

Kantian enlightenment and morality in formulating the maxim of what ought to be right or wrong, just and unjust, moral and immoral action performed by the person is heavily dependent on an assumption of human freedom. In very general terms, Kant's morality is surrounded in terms freedom and autonomy of the will, of which human reason is the source of origin. It assumes that all rational beings have the same rational capacity to act freely in accordance with a universal moral law. Thus, Kant offers a new conception of freedom which allows one's autonomy to be actualized in its actual form of freedom. Kant's conception of freedom lies at the heart of his theory of morality. In order to understand what is freedom and how it plays an important role in formulating the notion of morality and justice, it is important to grasp that Kant does not endorse that the notion of freedom as lack of constraints on one's actions. Instead, his concern is that freedom as subjection to no other laws than those which a person gives to himself, either alone or along with others. According to Kant, "to be free is not to lack constraints on one's actions, but to be independent of the constraints imposed by the arbitrary wills of others"[29].

Kant believed that the only grounds we have to attribute to freedom of will come from morality that can be possible through rationally governed individual. Kant's assumption is that human beings are categorically equal to one another by nature as a noumenal matter of free will. Though, people differ in capabilities. Kant builds his entire moral theory as well as his theory of justice based on the foundation provided by the assumption that man regarded as a homo noumenon is free. He argues that, by reasoning from that postulate, we can arrive at a single supreme principle of morality, which he calls the categorical imperative which is deduced from free will.

In *Groundwork of Metaphysic of Morals*, Kant claims that morality follows from the concept of freedom and gives a holistic explanation of the concept of free will:

> As Will is a kind of causality of living beings so far as they are rational, freedom would be that property of this causality by which it can be effective independently of foreign causes determining it, just as natural necessity is the property of the causality of all irrational beings by which they are determined to activity by the influence of foreign causes. The preceding definition of freedom is negative and therefore affords no insight into its essence. But a positive concept of freedom flows from it which is so much the richer and more fruitful. Since the concept of a causality entails that of laws according to which something, i.e., the effect, must be established through something else which we call cause, it follows that freedom is by no means lawless even though it is not a property of the will according to laws of nature. Rather, it

> must be causality according to immutable laws, but of a particular kind. Otherwise a free will would be an absurdity[30].

According to Kant, freedom is something real in human nature and we must presuppose free will if we want to think of a being as rational.

For Kant freedom is guided through autonomy of will. "Free will is nothing but autonomy of the will is self-legislative. To escape the heteronomy of will, man acts in accordance with a law he gives himself. The only rational law man can abide is the categorical imperative"[31]. Free will acts in accordance with moral reasoning and that's why individuals distinguish themselves from other life forms, and reach to some conclusions about rightness or wrongness of moral actions. This habit of moral reasoning occurs in the noumenal realm, and provides individuals with some understanding of the categorical imperative. The sense of distinguish between just and unjust action is evident through rational comprehension of the universal law which aims to protect freedom. And, since freedom, specifically freedom to exercise one's own will is the constituent feature of the noumenalrealm and its primary concern of right and moral. Therefore, the Kantian perception of free will is more specifically adherence to the morality of the categorical imperative. Freedom is duty. In his formulation, the laws of duty are derived from free will which consists in obeying self-imposed laws. The performance of an action is a duty, not when it seeks to attain an object of inclination, but when it is done upon the maxim which can become a universal law.

A free will and a will is subject to moral laws are one in the same. Rational law, come about through pure practical reason, is the only way to escape heteronomy. Practical reason not only gives principles to itself but also always acts according to them. It is concerned with the determining factors of the *will*. The *will* is causally connected with the conception of freedom. Practical reason determines the will and gives it objective reality in the sense that the will and the conception of freedom are given by practical reason to itself. This is what Kant wants to establish in his moral theory, by defining,

> Morality is in terms of acting from practical reason. Kant claims that since every human being has practical reason, everyone is a

> moral agent by his or her own nature and has a natural capacity to act morally. Acting morally means acting in accordance with universal moral laws or those maxims an agent can will as universal laws[32].

The universality of a moral action, Kant seems to claim, should be determined by the principle of the categorical imperative, the supreme moral principle.

Kant divides the self into the noumenal and the phenomenal, in which only the noumenal realm is indicative of true reality. The noumenal is the realm of freedom, the being-in-itself, that which is considered real, free, and universal.

> The will is thought of as a faculty of determining itself into action in accordance with the representation of certain laws, and such a faculty can be found only in rational beings. Now what serves the will as the objective ground of its self-determination is an end; and if this end is given by reason alone, then it must be equally valid for all rational beings[33].

Kant's emphasis on the freedom of the will means that understanding is based in the autonomy of the will and its ability to legislate that which is equally applicable to all others. "Autonomy of the will is the property that the will of being a law to itself independently of any property of the objects of volition"[34]. Autonomy lies in acting on the maxim of self-imposed laws. For instance, an individual can become autonomous if and only if he or she can act on self-imposed maxims rather than imposed by others maxim. Kant continues,

> The moral imperative must therefore abstract from every object to such an extent that no object has any influence at all on the will, so that practical reason or the will may not merely minister to an interest not belonging to it but may merely show its own commanding authority as the supreme legislation[35].

Kant further says,

> The phenomenal is the determined realm of appearance and only in the phenomenal realm is there diversity of opinions, feelings; needs and desires and thus legislation should not be constructed on phenomenal self of feelings, needs, and so on. But legislation

> can be possible on noumenal self because it is governed through free will and rationality whose effect is an end. Therefore the subjective ground of desire is the incentive; the objective ground of volition is the motive. Hence there arises the distinction between subjective ends which rest on incentives and objective ends which depend on motives valid for every rational being. Practical principles are formal when they abstract from all subjective ends; they are material, however, when they are founded upon subjective ends, and hence upon certain incentives[36].

Kant is clear that subjective ends are not valid for all beings and therefore cannot be considered when making claims about the rightness and justness of moral actions. The reasoning for this surely rests on the idea of equality for all rational creatures, but it neglects much of what it means to be human. Indeed, Kant argues that individuals should wish to be free from such subjective ends, since they cannot contribute to our moral reasoning and they do not distinguish us from other non-rational creatures. Kant argues that through moral reasoning, individuals distinguish themselves from enlightened and just to ignorant and unjust individual who can come up to some conclusions about the rightness or wrongness of moral actions. This moral reasoning occurs in the noumenal realm, and provides individuals free will with some understanding of the categorical imperative.

Kant defines "free will as a kind of causality or a power of causal action belonging to living beings so far as they are rational. To describe such a will as free would be to say that it can act causally without being caused to do so by something other than itself"[37]. Since free will in terms of practical reason is a self-legislator, it should follow its own commands. It should not act for an inclination or passion or law which is not given by it to itself. When practical reason is free from passions and inclinations, it only has laws or, in practical terms, maxims as moral laws. Free will is always law oriented but this law is not imposed on it by something other than itself. If laws would be other than itself then they would merely the laws of natural necessity. Therefor the free will is the principle of moral laws and it will act under moral laws that what ought to be just.

Thus according to Kant, freedom plays a key role in reason-based moral determination. The human will is directly determined by moral law because it has freedom as an inherent virtue. On Kant's view,

> Freedom plays its role both negatively and positively. In the negative sense, the principle of morality consists in freedom from all desired objects. It also consists in the determination of choice of universal legislation which a maxim must be capable of making. In the positive sense, freedom is the intrinsic legislation of pure and practical reason. Based on this the moral law expresses nothing else than the autonomy of the pure practical reason, i.e., freedom. This autonomy or freedom is itself the formal condition of all maxims, under which alone they can all agree with the supreme practical law.[38]

Kant thinks that reason functions under the presupposition that it is free negatively and positively as well. When it is determined by outside influences such as desires and inclination, and others interest rather than its own principle that is guided through morality then free will act negatively and the action done under this condition would be unjust. On the other hand, free will act positively if freedom is guided through the principle of own rationality and so called principle of morality then that freedom is just. As freedom is an inherent element of the nature of human reason. It determines universal moral law and helps the will in realizing its autonomy in thinking, legislating and acting. Now the question arises why freedom is a necessary presupposition of morality and enlightenment to develop the principle of universal maxim in Kant's philosophy?

Free will is very important because if one did not have freedom one would not be enlightened and just towards oneself and society. But this free will should rationally guide so far then that individual can become enlightened and just for himself and for the society. It is important because without it one would be controlled and would not have free will over one's own thinking willing and acting. On the other hand, if individual would possess his free will rationally without external forces like desires then he or she can apply laws of categorical imperative so that his or her maxim can become the universal law of morality and justice such as universal law of autonomy. Every individual needs freedom to express themselves and find their way in life to live better, enlightened and just. But this freedom exist in the will of rational being because they regard themselves as capable of acting on his own rational principle and this way they can regard their will as their own. Therefore every rational being must presuppose his will to be free. In this way free will is a prerequisite of all just actions.

Therefore, we can say that Kant's notion of morality and its maxims is based on the autonomy of will because once individuals acquire habit of autonomy in their willing, feeling and thinking then they act on that maxim which ought to be universalise. Thus, for Kant just and moral act can be performed through autonomy of the will.

Kant formulates his normative principles in the form of Categorical Imperative. The categorical imperative effectively illustrates the central characteristic of Kant's famous deontological ethics, because it provides a methodology for assessing the moral quality of one's actions by suggesting a unified principle of conduct. An imperative commands us. Such a command can be hypothetical or categorical. Now we can contrast the categorical imperative with what Kant calls hypothetical imperatives. "An imperative, or command, is hypothetical if its applicability to persons is contingent on the particular aspirations, intentions, or objectives they happen to adopt. It can also know as conditional imperative"[39]. For instance, if I want to become a musician, then it is a hypothetical imperative for me to pursue the necessary means to achieve the dreams to be a musician by practicing it. In this act I am not under moral obligation to realize this dream and many other people do not share it. So particular hypothetical imperative does not apply to others and applies to me only insofar as I maintain my aspiration. In contrast, categorical imperatives ought to adopt by every person. And every rational person applies with greater force than hypothetical imperatives. If any conict arises due to disagreement between two then the categorical imperative takes priority. Although Kant formulated the categorical imperative in reality is one and only one categorical imperative exists. That imperative is in one of its formulations is: "Act only according to that maxim whereby you can at the same time wills that it should become a universal law"[40]. For Kant, the insight of moral and just action is derived from this single command. For example, i ought never to act unjust or wrong except in in such a way that I can also will that my maxim of action should become the universal law of just and right action.

It has often been misconceived that Kant's categorical imperative is a version of the Golden rule which is commonly formulated in the statement: "Do unto others as you would have them do unto you"[41]. It seems clear that these two statements are unconditional commands that ought to be fallow under all circumstances. "These are reexive in the sense that both demand that the person to whom they are addressed put himself or herself in the place of another and consider whether a contemplated action would be acceptable to him or herself in that hypothetical circumstance"[42]. Both statements are intended to apply universally to all human beings. However, Kant's statement about categorical imperative differs from the Golden rule.

> The process of reection Kant demands that we undergo resembles the process commanded in the Golden rule, but it is more complex, more abstract, and more generalized. The Golden rule is intended to apply to discrete actions. It demands from its addressee to consider how he or she would want others to act toward him or her. Although the categorical imperative also applies to discrete actions, it does so through maxims[43].

As we know that maxims are rules of action and individuals adopt it in pursuit of the objectives purposes and they intended to choose in fact asks us to judge a maxims not on the basis of what we would want to happen to us but we consider that maxim which fulfils the condition of universality. While, in the Golden rule is guided through order not accordance with the subjective maxim of free will.

Kant's categorical commands an imperative which binds all of us irrespective of our particular desire and lies at the root of morality. Morality is the only law that harmonised all human being into one law that deduced from categorical imperative. Then question arises from what source such universal law-that spring forth into whole. It is the moral principle derived from our practical reason regulates our action and maxim in two aspects namely, the matter and the form. Kant says,

> If a rational being can think of its maxims as a universal law, he can do so only by considering them as principles which contain the determining grounds of the will be cause of their form and not because of their matter. The material of a practical principle is object of the will. This object either as the determining ground of the will or it is not. If it is, then the rule of the will is subject to an empirical condition (to the relation of the determining idea to feelings of pleasure, or displeasure), and therefore, it is not a practical law. If all material of law i.e. every object of the will is considered as a ground of its determination, is abstracted from it, nothing remains except the mere form of giving universal law. Therefore a rational being either cannot think of his subjective maxim as a universal laws or he must suppose that their mere form, through which they are fitted for being universal laws, is alone that which makes them a practical law[44].

The matter is the object of the will and desire. For Kant if this matter were the determining basis of the will, then any maxim would be subject to an empirical condition. Such kind of maxim cannot compatible with universal laws. For him, content in the formulation of universal law is derived from the very concept of a categorical imperative which essentially involves universality. The categorical imperative is a universal law and as such it applies to all of us. .

Kant writes,

> If I think of a categorical imperative, I know right away what it contains. For since this imperative contains, besides the law, only the necessity that the maxim conform to this law, while the law, as we have seen, contains no condition limiting it, there is nothing left over to which the maxim of action should conform except the universality of a law as such; and it is only this conformity that the imperative asserts to be necessary[45].

If the categorical imperative applies to all of us, then we must only act in accordance with maxims that can be willed to be universal law and this is the universal law of formulation: "Act only on that maxim by which you can at the same time will that it should become a universal law"[46]. The very concept of a categorical imperative is the concept of a universal law.

Kant grounds the basis for all morality in human being is born with the ability to rationally determine the moral quality of their actions. In other words, Kant regards the concept of the moral consciousness, generally referred as a conscience. It is the conscience which lies in the practical reason rather than theoretical reason of human being. It enables human beings to rationally determine the moral value of their behaviour. Therefore, he developed his famous formulation of the categorical imperative, which quickly became the exemplification of deontological ethical theory of morality. As we can easily be seen, the categorical imperative represents a way to formulate a moral code of conduct which intended to present the unifying rule for making moral decisions in any given situation.

In Kant's moral theory as a whole, the categorical imperative is in fact the basis for commands for both types of objects I mean the moral laws and the juridical laws or principle of justice. The distinction between these two types like actions on the one hand and maxims on the other is fundamental to a division between the two major branches of his moral theory. As applied to maxims and to the ends or objectives at which those maxims aim, a moral law are called ethical laws. "Ethical and so called moral principle constitutes prescriptions about the range of intentions and objectives so that we can rightfully or just fully adopt. As applied to actions, moral laws are called juridical laws"[47]. A juridical law is the principle of justice and it limits on people's conduct, not on their intentions or objectives. Kant's morality deals about both types of laws. His theory of morality, however, is concerned solely with ethical principle and with the inner sense that can be controlled through them.

Morality is a concept which treats every individual equally that is according to general principle or rule and this rule that binds all rational beings into one law is called categorical imperative. The categorical imperative is thus conceived as the fundamental principle of determining which principles can be objectively valid for the decisions of our will. When we say it is our duty to do something then we manifestly have in mind such a categorical demand or such an objectively valid principle. Hence, we can also say that on Kant's view the categorical imperative contains nothing but the concept of being under a possible moral obligation as such.

The moral law requires us always to treat others as ends-in-themselves and not merely as means, but it does not forbid us to use others so long as their fundamental autonomy is not abused. The principle of morality, Kant holds must be necessary, universal and sufficient to determine actions.

In his *Groundwork of the Metaphysic of Morals* Kant gives three such maxims of categorical imperative of morality. These three maxims ought to become the principle of morality if it can be universally applied to all rational human being. These are namely:

> "The Formula of the Universal Law, the Formula of Humanity and the Formula of the Kingdom of Ends"[48] To understand the first formulation of the categorical imperative and how it helps in formulating the principle of universality correctly, we need to understand Kant's conception of a maxim. In other words, it is an underlying, general rule to which we appeal when we perform actions. The first maxim: "So act that maxim of your will could always hold at the same time as a principle establishing universal law"[49]. This maxim shows that what is right is universal and that is expedient is not universal. Here, we arrive at what has become known as the Categorical Imperative. This claim is the moral law. Kant says,
>
> > The fundamental principle of morality thus presents itself to us in the form of 'categorical imperative': categorical, because we recognise that it demands are unconditional, but any imperative, because we recognise this law as something we ought to fallow, thus as a constraint, that is not something we always want to fallow. The concept of the categorical imperative is thus not identical to the concept of the fundamental principle of morality, but is rather the way in which fundamental principle of morality presents itself to us as beings who are rational but not purely rational[50].

It establishes how we ought to act so that it becomes universal law of morality. The demand of categorical imperative is unconditional. Every moral action is fundamentally a consciousness of the difference between duty and inclination, between doing what we ought to do whether we like to or not and doing merely what we like whether we ought to or not. The general nature of law is that it holds universally. We ought only to do that act which we can will to be a universal law. Kant illustrates this maxim through the example of breaking promises and committing suicide. A promise with the intention of not keeping it is not a duty, because the maxim underlying it is a device to extricate oneself from current difficulties. Moreover, if everyone makes false promises then promises will cease to be made. Thus, breaking promises cannot be universalized. Therefore, it is right to keep and wrong to break promise because it can't be universalised. Similarly is the case with suicide. To commit suicide out of disgust with life is not moral because it will lead to the annihilation of human life if it is universalized. On the other hand, if a man does not commit suicide even out of disgust with life, he would be adopting a maxim which can be followed by everyone. In other words, thinking whether or not one could consistently will the maxim of one's own actions to be adopted as a universal law of nature yields a decisive reason for acting or not acting.

> This representation of the moral law also stimulates a feeling of reverence in the agent, awe at his own power to resist nature and to posit ends, and respect for others who share this power. But reverence is a self-induced feeling, stimulated by reflection- this sets it apart from all other feelings, which are stimulated by sensation[51].

Kant states that while willing a maxim on the basis of universal law, it has to be maintained that the willing of this kind is always to be considered also as an absolute end and never simply as a means; because, "every rational being , exists as an end in itself, not merely as a means for arbitrary use of this or that will; he must in all his actions , whether they are directed to himself or to other rational beings, always be viewed at the same time as an end"[52]. The first formulation of categorical imperative deals about all principle of moral statements should be deduced from general law which apply to everyone under all circumstances.

Kant's second formulation of the categorical imperative is the Formula for Humanity such as: "Act in such a way that you always treat humanity, whether in your own person or in the person of any other, never simply as a means but always at the same time as an end"[53]. This maxim tells us that to treat humanity as of absolute worth. It shows that, it is morally just to treat humanity as an end rather as a means. The notion of morality demands that people should be treated equally as an end in themselves rather than as a means to some end. This feeling would promote equality and justice, because the first duty of justice is to never treat people as a means to one's own ends. But treating a person as an end themselves is to do more than respect this duty and it is also to assist them in achieving their moral lawful ends. It also means that we must always allow others free will to pursue their own goals without interference and treat them as rational beings capable of making their own choices.

The moral law requires us always to treat others as ends-in-themselves and not merely as means, but it does not prohibit us to use others so long as their fundamental autonomy is not abused. Our relations to other persons form the basis for a second formulation of the categorical imperative. We should treat other persons as ends in themselves rather than as means to other ends, which would be how we would treat them using means/end rationality. For Kant, "all our ethical duties arise from the obligation to make each human being's capacity for autonomous choice the condition of the value of every other end"[54]. A person can make himself enlightened and perfect because he or she can control on his will and make it conform to the moral law. But he or she can never make others autonomous and enlightened being because he cannot controls their wills. Moral will has to be cultivated by a person himself and not ought to be imposed on him by any other person. Perfection and enlightenment is to be achieved and not to be given. So all that a person can do for others enlightenment and morality is to bring the circumstances that are conducive to their maturity to become moral and enlightened. To regard every rational being as an end in itself and never as a means is to treat them with dignity and equal worth is indeed a great contribution of Kant in moral philosophy.

The third formulation of the categorical imperative is the formula of the kingdom of ends: "So act as if you were through your maxim a law making member of a kingdom of ends"[55]. It shows that, act as if your maxims would harmonize with a kingdom of ends. This means that the action should be consistent or universal with a world in which people are treated as end in themselves. It is a harmony of ends in that its member, and act only on maxims that can meet everyone's consent and they respect one another as a rational self-determining agents. The maxim of kingdom of ends promotes a right and just society and we can say that the idea of intelligible world. Kant defines a kingdom as a "systematic union of different rational beings under common laws"[56]. Every rational being derives his actions from the maxim of universal law and in all his actions, he regards himself and other rational beings always as ends. In doing so, "there arises a systematic union of rational beings under common objective laws-that is a kingdom"[57]. Through the kingdom of ends, Kant attempts to bring out complete harmony between the maxim of universal law and the maxim of end-in itself.

Kant thinks that any action that violate the laws we make as universal legislators in a kingdom aimed at protecting the autonomy of all its subjects are morally impermissible. It is important to note that these laws are intended to govern the kingdom of ends, which is a realm with very specific features. Kant defines a kingdom as a "systematic union of different rational beings under common laws"[58]. Every rational being derives his actions from the maxim of universal law and in all his actions, he regards himself and other rational beings always as ends. In doing so, "there arises a systematic union of rational beings under common objective laws-that is a kingdom"[59]. Through the kingdom of ends, Kant attempts to bring out complete harmony between the maxim of universal law and the maxim of end-in itself. The kingdom of ends is an ideal society of enlightened and moral persons fallowing the moral law. In this each member is autonomous and sovereign and he or she imposes principle of categorical imperative upon himself or herself. In it each one realises own goodness and promoting the goodness of others also, in this way perfect harmony of each and every individual to cultivate mutual respect and good will.

Now the above three maxims of Kant's moral laws cannot be derived from the experience but they are *a priori* and derived from reason. And since reason belongs to the rational will, so these maxims are derived from the rational will. In Kant's view, moral responsibility lies in the willing alone because the consequences are dependent upon the laws of nature in the phenomenal world, willing is due to man's free rational nature. Acting through the rational will requires freedom. Kant asserted that "laws of freedom are self-imposed laws. Freedom lies in obeying self-imposed laws. Freedom, thus, belongs to the rational will because it is the rational will that is free"[60]. And since these laws are self-imposed, they express autonomy of will. Thus, we can say that the maxim of categorical imperative is the foundational and the supreme principle of morality. Now the question arise that what makes it so special that it become the foundational principle of morality? It is the foundational principle of morality given the practical policies of which we can think and act accordingly. It has unconditional, universal reason-giving force. It is the practical principle that gives every rational creature a good practical reason to act and does so independently of any other possible consideration for instance, desire and inclination. We can act according to these maxims and it commands via pure practical reason. In fact these three maxims of categorical imperative is the command that I ought never to act wrong or unjust so that it can never become the universal principle of morality.

Good will is deduced from categorical imperative. It gives the insight of absolute moral action that ought to be performed under all circumstances. Good will is nothing but the moral worth of acting from duty. As Kant says, "the only thing that is good without qualification or restriction is a good will"[61]. It states that a good will alone can be a good in all circumstances because it is unconditional and absolute good. The first section of the *Groundwork* begins with, "It is impossible to imagine anything at all in the world, or even beyond it, that can be morally worth without qualication except a good will"[62]. In his mature thought, Kant holds that the only truly good thing is good will, and the only truly pure motive for moral action is the rational determination of duty. He observes that only a good will is good without qualification and always good. A good will is good in itself, not just for what it produces. Kant's explanation and defence of this claim is followed by another related claim, that only actions performed out of duty have moral worth. A will is good if it acts from the sense of duty and other moral motives, and not just in conformity with duty, or not from inclination. To act from duty is to act out of respect for the moral law. Kant writes,

> A good will is manifested in acting for the sake of duty. Hence, if we have to understand human goodness, we must examine the concept of duty. Human goodness is most conspicuous in struggling against the obstacles placed in its way by unruly impulses, but it must not be thought that goodness as such consists in overcoming obstacles[63].

A person can acquire the habit of good will if his purpose of acting is for the sake of duty. The goodness of will, according to Kant, does not depend on the results it consequences rather it lies in the form of maxim which has a law for its own sake. It possesses universality and necessity, and is performed for its own sake. For instance, the maxim such as we ought to be just under all circumstances like duty for duty's sake.

Good will has fallowing characteristics and it is deduced from the Categorical Imperative namely: the first is that the only thing that is unconditionally good is the good will. Secondly, good will is a will that acts from duty alone. Thirdly, acting from duty alone consists not in acting from inclination and desire, but out of respect for the moral law alone i.e., doing the act for no other purpose than the morally right thing to do. Fourthly, every hypothetical principle requires that a person have a certain desire or inclination. Finally, we can deduce from the above argument the only unconditionally good thing is acting in accordance with the Categorical Imperative and that is the good will.

Good will also give the insight of absolute morality which ought to be universalised.

> Good will is the only thing of unconditional value is a good will argues that such a will manifests itself only in doing ones duty

> for its own sake, and then concludes that since doing duty for its own sake deprives the will of any object of desires as a reason for action, nothing is left as a possible principle of morality but the conformity of actions as much as with universal law[64].

The value of a good will and moral worth cannot secure certain valuable ends whether for our own or for others. Indeed, it is good and just under any condition; its goodness must not depend on any particular conditions. In Kant's terms, a good will is a will whose decisions are wholly determined by moral demands or by the moral law. In the same way, individuals will become intrinsically good and so that it ought to be universalising the one good will to other good will which gives the absolute and unconditional principle that morality ought to be maintained under all circumstances. Kant says, "good will is manifested in acting for the sake of duty"[65]. Kantian good will surrounded with duty. Therefore his insight of justice is based on duty also. Here, we can derive justice from the motive of duty such as an action is unjust, if it is done from inclination and self-intrust. On the other hand a human action is morally just if it is done for the sake of duty. Here we formulate the principle of justice from the morality of good will in Kantian context that an action ought to be just for the sake for the sake of justice.

In Kant's moral setting of the code of conduct is that the formula of autonomy which is derived from the formula of universal law and formula of kingdom of end. It states that all rational agents acts autonomously according to the rational principle of moral law that is C.I. "If every rational being act according to the rationality then the law which we are bound to obey must be product of our own will. In this way the idea of the will of every rational being as will which makes universal law"[66]. It shows that rational being ought to perform in such a way that can universalise every autonomous will to be right then this maxim ought to be the universal principle of morality.

The second principle of absolute moral action ought to derive from maxim. "Act in such a way that you always treat humanity, whether in your own person or in the person of any other, never simply as a means but always at the same time as an end"[67]. It cultivates the sense of equality and justice that every being has his or her own dignity and moral worth. So treat in a way that you always treat human being whether self and others never as a means that is immoral but always at the same time as an end and with complete dignity.

> It requires that humanity whether in oneself or in any anyone else must always be treated as an end and never merely as a means, requires that each one of us always respect the free choice and action of everyone else, and therefore act only on that maxims that could be accepted by everyone else as perceiving their capacity for free choice as well[68].

It shows that, it is moral to treat humanity as an end rather means. Treating equally every human being as equally free to adopt any subjective principle that any one of us is free to act upon must be followed. It is the equality in morality demands that people should be treated equally as an end in themselves rather than as a means to some an end.

Therefore, morality demands that each person should be treated equally as an end in himself or herself rather than as a means to some end. This feeling among people would promote equality and justice, because the first duty of morality is to never treat people as a means for one's own benefit. Though treating a person as an end in itself is to do more than respect this duty and it is also to assist them in achieving his or her moral ends. The idea of treating humanity as an end in itself is to treat each individual as an autonomous individual. An autonomous individual is capable of formulating his or her ends freely as well as in harmony with others. This harmonious attitude of each individual creates the third formulation of Kant's kingdom of ends. The third principle of moral action contributes in Kant's notion of just and moral society is the formula of the kingdom of ends. It states, "So act as if you were through your maxims a law making member of a kingdom of an ends"[69]. It shows that, act as if your maxims would harmonize with a kingdom of ends. The kingdom of ends promotes a just and moral society or an idea of intelligible world wherein every individual become enlightened and just so that we would live in enlightened age rather an age of enlightenment that what Kant's dream. Kant's just society ought to be when everyone performed their duties namely, juridical duties and ethical duties. The former is duty to oneself and the latter is duty to others. Ethical duties to oneself include both perfect and imperfect and also duties of respect to others. Kingdom of ends says that if everyone act just and universalise the maxim of categorical imperative then the society would become just society.

To bring this chapter to an end we can say that enlightenment and morality are complementary to each other. In fact both are two sides of same coin. At the one side enlightenment projects deals about individual's right, tolerance, autonomy and public and private reason which helps to acquire the image of just man. It is the enlightenment which helps the individual to come out from ignorant and unjust life to the authentic and autonomous life by the use of reason. It is the enlightenment which emphasised on the individual rights leads the habit of tolerance, autonomy; public and private reason helps in evolving the just man. However once individual reach to the stage of autonomy can construct the principle of morality for maintaining universality in the society. Enlightened people can act accordance with universal law of morality. Morality gives insight that how right, tolerance, autonomy and public and private reason ought to be shared by all with the help of unconditional principle of categorical imperative. Therefore, enlightenment opportunities that ought to be universally given to all humanity irrespective religion, caste, creed, and race. It gives the universal principle of right; autonomy, tolerance and freedom to use of public reason that ought to be applied equally by all rational being under all circumstances. It gives the foundation of absolute morality such as Good will which helps to construct the universal principle of morality i.e. universality in individuals autonomy and end in itself which leads to the kingdom of end.

Notes

1. Kant. *What is Enlightenment? in Kant on History*. p. 4.
2. Kant. *What is Enlightenment? in Kant on History*. p. 3.
3. *Ibid.,* p. 3.
4. Kant. *Critique of Judgment*. pp. 160-161.
5. *Ibid.,* p. 162.

6. Kant, Immanuel. *Enlightenment East and West*. p. 61.
7. Singh, *Freedom and Causation with Special Reference to Hegel's Overcoming of Kant.* p. 32.
8. *Ibid.,* p. 33.
9. Kant, "An Answer to the Question: What is Enlightenment?," p. 58.
10. *Ibid.,* p. 60.
11. Kant, An Answer to the Question: What Is Enlightenment?. p. 58-60.
12. Kant, "Enlightenment and Freedom," pp. 223-44.
13. *Ibid.,* p. 237.
14. Kant, *Science of Right*, p. 6.
15. Kant, *Groundwork of the Metaphysic of Morals.* p. 12.
16. *Ibid.,* p. 2.
17. Kant, *Science of Right.* p. 12.
18. Onora O'Neill,*Constructions of Reason: Explorations of Kant's Practical Philosophy*. p. 50.
19. *Ibid.,* p. 28.
20. Noggle, "Kantian Respect and Particular Person". p. 450.
21. Kant, *Groundwork of the Metaphysic of Morals,* p. 54-55.
22. Kant, *Critique of Practical Reason,* p. 24.
23. Kant, "An Answer to the Question: What is enlightenment?,". p. 60.
24. *Ibid.,* p. 63.
25. Peterson Jonathan, "Enlightenment and Freedom," p. 228.
26. *Ibid.,* p. 228.
27. Peterson Jonathan, "Enlightenment and Freedom," p. 228.
28. Kant, *Critique of Practical Reason*. p. 29.
29. Kant, *The Moral Law: Groundwork of the Metaphysic of Morals.* p. 41.
30. Kant, *The Moral Law: Groundwork of the Metaphysic of Morals.* p. 39.
31. *Ibid.,* p. 49.
32. Kant, *Critique of Practical Reason*. pp. 28-29.
33. Kant, *The Moral Law: Groundwork of the Metaphysic of Morals.* p. 35.
34. *Ibid.,* p. 44.
35. *Ibid.,* p. 45.
36. *Ibid.,* p. 35.
37. *Ibid.,* p. 41.
38. *Ibid.,* p. 42.
39. Kant, *The Moral Law: Groundwork of the Metaphysic of Morals.* p. 45.
40. *Ibid.,* p. 67.
41. Johnston, David, , "Kant's theory of justice," pp. 151-153.

42. *Ibid.,* p. 152.
43. *Ibid.,* p. 153.
44. Kant, *Critique of Practical Reason,* p. 26.
45. Kant, *The Moral Law: Groundwork of the Metaphysic of Morals.* p. 37.
46. *Ibid.,* p. 67.
47. *Ibid.,* p.142.
48. *Ibid.,* p.67-69.
49. Kant. *Critique of Practical Reason*, p. 30.
50. Guyer, Paul. *Kant.* p. 180.
51. *Ibid.,* p. 69.
52. *Ibid.,* p. 95.
53. *Ibid.,* p. 32.
54. Christine M, *The Sources of Normativity.* p. 331.
55. Kant, *The Moral Law: Groundwork of the Metaphysic of Morals.* p. 34.
56. *Ibid.,* p. 95.
57. *Ibid.,* p. 96.
58. *Ibid.,* p. 95.
59. *Ibid.,* p. 96.
60. *Ibid.,* p. 17.
61. Thomas E, ed. *The Blackwell Guide to Kant's Ethics.* p. 18.
62. Kant, *The Moral Law: Groundwork of the Metaphysic of Morals.* p. 19.
63. *Ibid.,* p. 18.
64. Guyer, Paul. *Kant.* p. 177.
65. Kant, *The Moral Law: Groundwork of the Metaphysic of Morals.* p. 18.
66. Thomas.ed.*The Blackwell Guide to Kant's Ethics.* p. 52.
67. *Ibid.,* p. 58.
68. Paul, Guyer. *Kant.* p. 190-94.
69. Kant, *The Moral Law: Groundwork of the Metaphysic of Morals.* p. 100-101.

Chapter - 3

Kant on Justice

In this chapter, I will develop the notion of justice in Kant's philosophy with reference to enlightenment rationality and morality. Since enlightenment implies the freedom to use one's own understanding to become autonomous and sovereign. Kant's theory of justice implies that one should have courage to use his or her freedom and rationality on the one hand and morality on the other hand to become just as well as moral. I will also formulate how morality becomes the foundation of Kant's theory of justice. Then I will develop a principle of justice that protects individual freedom and equality, formulated by the method of social contract or social agreement in terms of public reason.

In the European modernity, it is the enlightenment rationality of Kant that has played the most important role in formulating the notion of universal justice. It is the enlightenment rationality which helps us to become autonomous and sovereign in creating a just society. It inculcates the attitude to become autonomous and sovereign on the famous maxim "sapereaude" or have courage to use your own understanding to become just man"[1]. In formulating the theory of justice in Kantian perspective, enlightenment rationality plays an important role because it is the stage at which human beings departs from his immaturity, prejudices and partial nature and is able to use one's own understanding without the guidance of another. It is the stage at which human being recognizes his or her freedom, rationality, rights, autonomy and sovereignty and acts on self-imposed law which is compatible with others to acquire the image of a just man. It develops rationality to the extent that individuals becomes autonomous and get rid of restraints from tradition and construct his or her self-imposed principle that can fulfil the condition of categorical imperative. It is the enlightened person who comes out from others imposed laws and makes self-imposed laws that can consistently applied to become just by using reason and understanding.

Kant's sense of justice is constructed on the principle of autonomy of will, universality, and end in itself. It emphasises on human freedom, equality, and fraternity for all human being. It gives some insight of justice to make people autonomous and to use their right, tolerance, and autonomy so that everyone ought to become enlightened and reach to the age of enlightenment. Kant's justice emphasized on universal principle for freedom, right, equality, and autonomy on which individual, state, government, country functions or acts are reasonably just which ought to be universal.

Kant's notion of absolute justice is a universal norm of justice that enables us in assessing how individuals and societies ought to be fair and just. In Kantian perspective, justice is the means to achieve absolute principle of justice, that is, morality which is an end in itself. That's why Kant's vision of absolute justice is deduced from the morality which ought to be just under all circumstances. It is the morality which gives some insights to be just by using one's freedom which can coexist with others freedom.

Kant's principle of justice is to protect individual freedom and equality. This will be followed by the social contract or social agreement in terms of public reason. There will be an attempt to formulate proper public consent or social agreement or social contract to protect individual freedom, rights, autonomy etc. Kant's social contract turns out to be the most appropriate normative model for the vision of the justice in today's world. It helps to protect and safeguard individual freedom and equality by single principle which unites into single principle i.e. categorical imperative to reach to the absolute justice.

In order to organise my discussion, I shall divide it into the fallowing three parts:

Part 1: Morality as a foundation of justice.

Part 2: Justice as a protection of individual freedom and equality.

Part 3: Justice and Social Contract.

Before I come to Part1of the chapter I would like to say that justice is a concept, which deals with the fact that people should be treated fairly concerning their rights, freedom, need and choices. Its main concern is the proper ordering of freedom and right, autonomy and use of public reason within a society. As a concept it has been subject to philosophical debates on moral, legal, religious and human right issues throughout history. The diversity of its connotation makes it difficult to lay down the precise meaning of justice. It is dynamic in nature and its implication varies with respect to time and situation with reference to legal, political, economic, and social and ethical.

Part - I

Morality as a Foundation of Justice

Kant's morality is the foundational pillar in formulating the principle of absolute justice. In absolute justice, every principle is evaluated by the categorical imperative. It is the morality which gives the insight of absolute justice that how individual's autonomy, right, equality, and toleration ought to be given among all human beings irrespective of any differences. For him, morality is the end and justice is the means which helps to achieve this end. "Justice is not merely one important value among others, to be weighed and considered as the occasion requires, but rather the means by which values are weighed and assessed"[2].

On Kant's view, the concept of utility cannot be a foundation for absolute justice. Kant was the first one who rejected the assumption of utility can helps to formulate the universal principle of justice. "Kant empathetically rejected the assumption that the promotion of human enjoyment or happiness can ever serve as a foundation for sound ideas about justice"[3]. Kant's morality and its absolute justice criticize utilitarianism because it is unreliable in the way that no empirical foundation can secure the primacy of justice and sanctity of individual rights. Kant says, "Justice is concerned simply with the problem of harmonizing individual wills by giving them universal autonomy compatible with similar autonomy for others"[4]. In fact, same view was given by J.S. Mill in terms of maximum liberty which can be compatible with similar liberty for others but Kant's central concept was autonomy not utility. Utilitarianism took shape as the utility based conception of justice. Kant's belief that human beings are free, rational, and responsible is the foundation of all sound principle of morality and justice. Kant repeatedly asserts two arguments in refutation of the notion that utility can never serve as appropriate basis for reasoning about morality and justice. As Sandel says,

> Any conclusions we might reach by reasoning from the ground of utility would be uncertain. This is the central point of his trusteeship example. Kant argues that the trustee who chooses to decide how to dispose of the estate on the basis of utilitarian consequences would be compelled to estimate the consequences of every possible disposition. In contrast, he argues, the trustee who chooses to do what Kant believes duty requires need have no doubt about the rightful course of action[5].

The notion of justice in Kant also argues that "the sound theory of morality cannot be based on happiness because the causes of happiness vary from person to person, so that only the individual affected is well situated to decide how best to pursue his or her happiness"[6]. Kant believes that the utilitarian principle of happiness cannot be universalized because each person's happiness depends on his or her experience of what brings them joy. For instance, if A's interest is in playing football and B's interest is in studying then A will find his or her joy or happiness in playing football and B's happiness will depend on how well he or she studies. The notion of happiness varies from person to person, Kant argues. Individuals have different views on the empirical end of happiness and their subjective desires can be brought neither under any common principle nor under any external law harmonising with the freedom of everyone.

In Kant's view, any conclusion we might reach by the ground of utility would not be evaluated by the general principle of categorical imperative and therefore, it would be unjust. If a principle that presupposes certain desires and inclination would be conditional and our desires and means of satisfying them vary both between individual to individual. Thus all principle which assumes an object of desires and inclination as the determining ground of the will are without exception empirical and furnish no universal laws. Kant argues that "no general or universal conclusion about morality can be reached on the basis of happiness as the precepts of morality must by nature be universal commanding every person in the same way and taking no account on inclinations that vary from person to person"[7]. It is moral and just for each human being to be allowed to pursue happiness in his or her own way and it is unjust to attempt to impose on human beings any particular conception of happiness.

As utility is the determining ground in the utilitarian principle to provide general welfare overrides justice rather it fulfils it. Kant's exception for human desires and inclination has been rejected because if the desire for utility were universally shared, it could not serve as basis for the universal moral law. As persons would differ in their conception of happiness and for any conception as regulative would impose on conception of others and in this way deny at least to some freedom to advance their own conceptions. It would create a society where some were coerced for the sake of others, rather than one where the needs of each is harmonised with the ends of all. Kant's criticism of utility based ideas about morality which underlies the conception of absolute justice and his interest of the conception of justice were alternative to those ideas.

Kant's absolute justice derived from universal principle of morality that is called categorical imperative which gives vision of what justice is and how it ought to be universalised. Justice consists in autonomy of one person that coexists with the autonomy of others so that it becomes universal law of autonomy. Kant says that,

> justice is an act externally so that free exercises of your personal will could be brought under general law together with the freedom of everyone- consummates the separation between law and justice on the one hand as concerned only with external behaviour, and morality on the other hand as concerned with inner life.[8]

This definition of justice shows that justice and morality are inseparable from each other. Both are like the two sides of the same coin, one is based on external and other is on internal life. Morality and justice are interrelated concepts. While morality deals with inner behaviour, justice deals with outer behaviour of individual. For Kant, absolute justice is a moral concept. It treats individuals equally, that is, according to general principle of categorical imperative which binds all rational beings under one law.

The moral principle of justice is made necessary by its foundational priority. The vision of Kant's justice underlying in morality are independently derived from any condition, so that the principle is ought to universalise under all circumstances. "The moral law and the principle of justice are not implicated in various contingent interests and ends; it does not presuppose any particular conception of good"[9]. Its basis is prior to all empirical ends and the purpose of justice is to attain an end in itself and objective reality so that it ought to be shared by all. In other words we can say that the basis of morality and justice is to be found in the hands of subject's will or autonomous being and not the object of practical reason, because a rational subject is capable of autonomous will to construct the principle of justice. Thus, autonomous will can only give rise to the conception of absolute justice. Only such an enlightened and moral person whose will is autonomous can elevate himself as a part of the world of inequality and injustices and enables himself to participate in an ideal, unconditioned realm. This is called Kant's kingdom of ends where individual is wholly impartial and independent of desire and social inclination and detach himself by the contingencies of circumstances. In this way every individual ought to act in such a way that their action fulfils the purpose of universal moral law that is called categorical imperative based on the principle of universality, end in itself, kingdom of ends and finally the good will. Therefore, Kant's absolute justice brought out from the universal principle of morality in the form of categorical imperative which commands what is to be just and moral and how justice ought to be. It also command how freedom, autonomy, human rights, toleration, use of public and private reason ought to be universalise to achieve an absolute justice for all. Therefore, moral principle and its universal justice does not deal with any empirical end but rather an enlightened and moral being acts himself in such a way so that it reaches at the stage of universal principle of categorical imperative. The maxims of categorical imperative must be made the ground for just action.

Kant's notion of justice is based on his deontological view. Kant argues that the right of the individual has primacy over the good. Michael, J Sandel says in *Liberalism and the Limits of justice*,

> The primacy of justice describes not only a moral priority but also a privileged from justification; the right is prior to the good not only in that its claims take precedence, but also in that its principle are independently derived. This means that, unlike other practical injections, principle of justice are just. The concern of justice is not privileged with the good rather justified in a way that does not depend on any particular vision of the good. To the contrary: given its independence status, the right constrains the good and sets its bounds. The concept of good and evil is not defined prior to the moral law, to which, it would seem, the former would have to serve as foundation; rather the concept of good and evil must be defined after and only by means of the law[10].

The right takes precedence over good because the principle of right is independently derived. The principle of justice does not depend on any particular form of goodness rather the right or moral constrains the good. The concept of good cannot be defined prior to the moral law but it must be defined only after the means of law based on the right and moral. For Kant justice comes from right and moral and it is prior to the question of what is good. In formulating the principle of justice one must bring morality before taking about good.

Let's see how three formulations of categorical imperative underlying vision of absolute justice are offered as evaluative tools to assess the maxim of individual's action as just or unjust. It states that enlightened persons ought to perform in such a way so that it contributes in formulating universal principle in Kant's justice. These are proposed as a principle of absolute justice that entails a universal moral code. ------Kantian notion of justice is looking for some insight to make people autonomous and sovereign so that they will act in such a way that it constructs the universal principle of justice. This ought to be universalised in formulating the universal principle of justice that concerns with the autonomy of one individual is to be compatible with others autonomy.

The universality of morality shapes the very foundation of absolute justice. Justice consists in the universal law of autonomy in which everyone acts in such a way so that it becomes the universal law of justice. Kant's notion of justice is concerned about universality of maxim that deals with how a justice ought to be. The principle of justice is deduced from the formula of universal law of categorical imperative: "so act that the maxim of your will could always hold at the same time through which you can as a principle establishing universal law"[11]. It is proposed that we ask ourselves whether the maxim by which we propose to guide our actions can simultaneously will that all others should act on. The point is to consider what we can consistently will, must be done, not only by ourselves but also by all others. In accepting and fallowing the categorical imperative we accept the moral reality and the maxim of absolute justice, and the possibility of moral and just community.

Thus, principle of absolute justice deduced from maxims as underlying guidelines principle of action proposes to guide the idea of absolute justice and its principle that can simultaneously will that all others ought to act and share. In this way in formulating principle of universal justice, perfect duties play an important role because it does not allows any exception in the interests of inclination.

For Kant duty is of two kinds, namely, perfect duty and imperfect duty. Perfect duty is towards self and imperfect duty is towards others. According to Kant,

> A perfect duty is one which admits of no exception in the interests of inclination. Under this heading the examples given are the ban on suicide and on making a false promise in order to receive a loan. We are not entitled to commit suicide because we have a strong inclination to do so, nor are we entitled to pay our debt to one man and not to another because we happen to like him better. In the case of imperfect duties the position is different: we are bound only to adopt the maxim of developing our talents and of helping others and we are to some extent entitled to decide

arbitrarily which talents we develop and which persons we will help[12].

Perfect and imperfect duties serve as the criteria for maxim of universality. Onara O'Neill writes,

> These two aspects of formula for universal law are to serve as the criteria for maxims of strict (or perfect), and of wide (or imperfect) duties. Kant brings duties of justice and of respect for self and others under the first heading, and duties of beneficence and self-development under the second[13].

Through perfect duties, enlightened being ought to bring duties of justice and of respect for self and others. On other hand, imperfect duties of beneficence and self-development also contribute in formulating the maxim of absolute justice. In this way universal principle of categorical imperative commands that enlightened persons ought to perform perfect duties not only in external sense but in inner sense as well. Therefore, the principle of universality states that enlightened persons ought to act on that maxim through perfect and imperfect duties which will become the universal principle of justice. However, "principle of justice could be fixed by constructing principle of obligation rather than of entitlement"[14]. As in the tradition of social contract approach, principle of justice gets formulated in obligation rather than entitlements. Kant's constructivist approach to justice lies in the principle of obligation and its reciprocal attitude of enlightened being. Thus, Kant's categorical imperative commands that every individual ought to perform the perfect and imperfect duties for maintaining just society.

Justice demands that action and institution not to be based on the principle of coercion, inequality, violence and deception because it cannot be universalized. A principle of coercion, whose enactment undercuts the individual's willing which cannot be universally implemented. Those who are at a given time the victims of coercion cannot act freely so cannot make coercion their own principle. Equally, action on a principle of violence or inequality damages or curtails the freedom of individuals to some extent. So it cannot be universally acted on. It shows that those principle of action that hinge on victimizing someone, whether by destroying, paralyzing and curtailing their capacities for enlightened moral agency for at least some time and in some ways, can be adopted by some but cannot be universally adopted. Therefore, justice is presupposed in universality of right, autonomy, toleration and other social opportunities to make individual sovereign to act on the universal maxim of action so that it becomes the principle of absolute justice.

Justice consists in individual's freedom, autonomy, right, and sovereignty and principle of justice is meant to give individuals freedom on the basis of moral law that ought to be universalised. "Justice is concerned simply with the maxim of harmonising individual wills by giving them maximum autonomy that ought to be compatible with similar autonomy for others"[15]. This maxim makes it clear that what is just or right is universal and what is unjust or expedient is not universal. Justice consists in maximum autonomy of will rather than heteronomy of will because latter cannot be harmonised with other's autonomy in formulating absolute principle. It consists in universality which determines all kinds of discrimination in the context of right, autonomy, toleration and private use of reason. It is unjust to deprive other's freedom and autonomy, because in that case the right of autonomy cannot be universalised. If it were made a universal rule then inequality in terms of autonomy has to be removed. The maxim makes it clear that it is unjust to curtail or not tolerate others freedom and autonomy, because it cannot become the universal principle of justice. And if this inequality would be removed then the autonomy of one would be compatible with others autonomy to fulfil certain condition of the universality. If intolerable attitude would be practiced by all persons then there would be no person left to tolerate other's freedom. That's why Kant's notion of justice states that to tolerate other's freedom in such a way that everyone else should tolerate each other under the same general condition. This is the first maxim of absolute justice that commands each enlightened and moral person to tolerate others freedom, autonomy, right and not to act in such a way that can curtail others freedom. Otherwise Kant's vision of justice in the form of universality would be unachievable.

Kant's vision of justice is looking for the principles of universal freedom, rights, autonomy, toleration and others human opportunities under the principle of universal law. Justice concerns in self-imposed laws by one enlightened person that ought to coexist with others self-imposed laws to formulate a universal law of justice that enables freedom, right, autonomy and respect for others right should universally manifested in the hands of all human being. The purpose of justice is to make people autonomous so that they can act according to the self-imposed maxims that coexists with others maxim to become universal principle of justice. These principles are deduced from the formula of universal principle of justice: "Act only on that maxim through which autonomy one compatible with the autonomy for all so that it can at the same time ought to become a universal law of autonomy"[16]. It deals with the principle of common autonomy on the basis of general law which apply to everyone under all circumstances. There should be no occasion under which an exception of injustice regarding discrimination on individual's autonomy is made.

The second maxims of categorical imperative, that is, 'end in itself' underlies the vision of absolute justice, consist in the notion of balanced reciprocity among human beings. Kant considered "all enlightened persons, regarded as *hominess noumena*, should be equally treated. For, he viewed balanced reciprocity as the basis of just relations among all people"[17]. The sense of justice can bring every members of the society reciprocally respect each other's freedom, right, toleration, and autonomy by refraining from violations of them. It is clear that the attitude of reciprocity plays an important role in just treatment. The sense of justice consists in the maxim of morality, Kant says, "man as an end-in-himself, i.e. he is never to be used merely as a means for someone[18]". This kind of maxim shows that treating humanity in terms of respect, dignity and moral worth is just rather as a means for others benefit. Justice demands that people should be treated equally as an end in themselves rather than means to some end. This rationality would promote equality and justice, because the first duty of justice is never to treat people as a means to one's own end. But treating persons as end in themselves is to do more than respect this duty and it is also to assist them in achieving their moral lawful ends.

> The categorical imperative in the maxim of end-in-itself states that in the order of ends, man and every rational being is an end

> in itself i.e. he is never to be used merely as a means for someone (even for God) without at the same time being himself an end, and that thus the humanity in our person must itself be holy to us, because man is subject to the moral law and therefore to the subject to that which is of itself holy and it is only on account of this and in agreement with this that anything can be called holy[19].

The attitude towards end in itself is deduced from the categorical imperative based on the autonomy of a person's will as a free will which ought to be compatible with treating others as an autonomous being. It purports to tell enlightened individuals what they ought to do to maintain harmony and justice among individual by respecting their dignity as a human being. It states that willing a just maxim on the basis of universal law, it has to be maintained that the willing of this kind is always to be considered as an absolute end and never simply as a means, because, ".....every enlightened being, exists as an end in itself, not merely as a means for arbitrary use of will; he must in all his actions, whether they are directed to himself or to other beings always viewed as the same time as an end"[20].

The moral law in the form of perfect and imperfect duties command us always to treat others as an end in themselves or equal absolute worth not merely as a means or worth for the sake of something else. However this maxim does not forbid us to use others enlightened being so long as their fundamental autonomy is not curtailed and abused by others. Our equal and just relation to others form the matter or basis for the principle of absolute justice. It gives the matter of universal principle of justice that how to treat and respect others with dignity as an objective reality rather as a subjective reality so that it ought to universalized. The aim of absolute justice would be achieved when every enlightened being treats other with respect and dignity and never tried to use them for the sake of own ends. For example, if I am treating others as forced labour and coerce them to do what I want them to do then I am treating them as a means for the sake of my own needs is unjust and cannot be universalized. The maxim of treating people as an end in themselves is to treat them with respect and dignity which contributes to absolute justice.

The third principle of categorical imperative underlies the sense of justice in the formula of the kingdom of ends. Kant defines "kingdom as a systematic union of different rational beings under common laws"[21]. In this enlightened society, every enlightened being derives their action from the maxim of universal law and considers himself and others in this society as an end not as means to maintain justice and harmony. It attempts to bring out complete justice and harmony between the maxim of universal law and the maxim of end in itself which commands rational being in the maxim: "So act as if you were through your maxims a law making member of a kingdom of an ends"[22]. It shows that act in such a way so that your maxims would harmonize with a kingdom of ends. This means that the action should be consistent with universal law in which people are treated as end in themselves. It is a harmony of ends in that its member can act only on the maxims that can meet everyone's consent and they respect one another as a rational self-determining agent. The kingdom of ends promotes a just society or an idea of intelligible world wherein every individual acts as an enlightened being so that we would live in enlightened age or society. The kingdom of ends promotes a just society or an idea of intelligible world wherein every individual becomes enlightened and just. Kant's just society ought to be realized when everyone performed their duties namely, ethical duties and juridical duties. The former is duty to oneself and the latter is duty to others. Ethical duties to oneself include both perfect and imperfect and also duties of respect to others. Kingdom of ends says that if everyone acts justly and universalise the maxim of categorical imperative then the society would become a just society.

In the kingdom of ends, enlightened being vanishes all kind of prejudices and discrimination because they combine the principle of universal law and end in itself to construct the common laws that unites every human being. The former specifying the form that maxim of duty must have and latter determining matter or end that they must have. It creates such society wherein the particular objects of desire that autonomous being pursues are constrained by the universally willed categorical imperative.

In this way enlightened person construct the principle of justice that could be absolute in nature. In fact, they realized that everything in nature works accordance with laws. Therefore, it is moral obligation to fallow the laws of categorical imperative to maintain a just society wherein enlightened person does not consider himself as a part of sensible world from which their inclinations and heteronomous moral principles derive as a result of natural causality. On the other hand they can think of themselves as belonging to an "intelligible world from which their duties and autonomous moral principles derive as a result of the moral law"[23].

Now, I shall find how categorical imperative commands that justice ought to be and contributes in the notion of absolute justice. In Kant's absolute justice enlightened and moral being formulate the principle of justice on the basis of two maxim of universality and end in itself which represent categorical imperative in the form of autonomous will rather heteronomous consideration and that is the point from which enlightened person construct the sense of justice for all. The goal of justice is to find principles of justice to which free and equal citizens could or should rationally agree and act accordance with perfect and imperfect duties to bring justice for himself and others.

Finally, Good will gives the vision of absolute justice that how human being should be just and moral under all circumstances. The sense of good will inculcate the habit of individual to act on the maxim of categorical imperative. It states that justice is self-imposed i.e. law of justice is democratically self-imposed. It comes once individual act on the maxim of morality namely universality and end in itself, can acquire the nature of good will. Every enlightened being must bring perfect and imperfect duty to acquire the nature of good will. As we know that autonomy is good if it use in justified ways. It can also be unjust for example an enlightened person cannot act on the maxim of universality and end in itself. Kant argues that only one thing is good in and of itself unconditionally, which is a 'good will' which implies that the will of a person who wants to do just action. It gives the idea that how to formulate a maxim that can bring absolute justice.

> It is unconditionally good and the absolutely good if it cannot be evil- i.e., if its maxim when made into a universal law can never be variance with itself. This principle is therefore also its supreme

principle: Act always on the maxim whose universality as a law you can at the same time will[24].

This is the one principle on which a will can never be unjust and inconsistent with itself and emphasized an imperative which is always categorical and just because it is compatible with universal principle of justice.

Good will is one of the foundational pillars in Kant's theory of justice. It gives the vision of absolute justice that can be applied under all circumstances. The principles of justice are self-imposed laws for Kant. Justice consists in obeying self-imposed laws which are coexistent with others rational self-imposed laws to fulfil the condition of universality and end in itself. Justice belongs to rational will because it is the rational will would autonomous and act on self-imposed laws. Kant believes, "a free and good will act under the laws, but these laws could not be imposed on it by something other than itself; for if they were, they would merely be laws of necessity. If the laws of freedom cannot be other imposed they must be self-imposed"[25]. That is to say autonomy is identical with goodness and sense of justice. It may be said that Kant's absolute justice is possible with good will because it is the reason and moral obligation states laws in accordance with which one ought to act just.

The good will underlies the vision of justice that can be univeralisable for all human being irrespective of any differences. It can bring when autonomous person can act according to the universal principle of amorality i.e. categorical imperative. It is the only absolutely good. A will is good not because of its effects but in itself and for itself. An action is morally just if its motive is moral if and only if it is promoted by consciousness of duty. Good will is the only jewel that shines intrinsically. Hence we have an insight of absolute justice from the notion of good will. For instance, right, tolerance, autonomy, equality fraternity, use of public reason cannot be unconditionally worth. Right and autonomy can be misused by bad will; they are morally just if it is use by the good will. We can take an example, suppose a nation can construct a good will in formulating a universal principle which promotes peace and harmony among all nations. Therefore it demands that justice consists in autonomy of all human being so that their subjective principle or maxims unite into such a way that shows universal justice.

Thus, Kant's morality is the foundational pillar in formulating the principle of absolute justice in a well ordered society. In formulating the principle justice, morality represents a conception of justice that how justice ought to be. It also inculcates the habit in individual to act in the conformity of categorical imperative to accept an ideal of the person and in acting from these principles we realize an ideal such as universality, end in itself, and the kingdom of ends. It is the enlightened and moral person who forms a just society in the form of kingdom of end. The just society reaches at the notion of well-ordered society wherein every enlightened being would be free and equal to each other. In Kant's just society it is regulated with a single law, that is, the law of categorical imperative which commands a maxim that act in such a way so that it becomes the principle of justice.

Part - II

Justice as a Protection of Individual Freedom and Equality

In Kant's theory of justice, freedom plays an important role. Kant's vision of justice revolves around the idea of individual freedom and the principle of justice is meant to regulate and safeguard individual liberty. It is a synthesis of individual's freedom and equality. It reconciles the contradiction and conflict of individual's freedom and equality and formulates the universal principle of freedom. Regarding justice, the very basic question arises that why should individual's freedom be protected? Why should freedom and liberty be distributed equally among all individuals? The sense of justice implies that individual's freedom and liberty in society should be regulated by rational principle. It is the sense of justice that recognizes the dignity of human being. It demands that each individual should be treated as an end in itself and not as a means to some end. In this way all individuals should be treated as equal to each other. No one ought to be treated unequal in terms of freedom, autonomy, right and other social opportunities.

In Kant's view, autonomy is one of the important concerns of justice. Everyone ought to have equal freedom to become autonomous and sovereign. Through it, they can acquire the capacity for self-imposed moral law. Autonomous being set their self-imposed laws or own standards of conduct as distinct from the demands made by their desires, and is able to decide and act on these standards. Kant says that,

> … autonomy is the supreme principle of morality. Autonomy of the will is that property by which it is a law to itself independent of any property of the object of its volition. The principle of autonomy then is; always to choose that the same volition shall comprehend the maxim of our choice as a universal law"[26].

Autonomy is one of the concerns of justice and it is possible only if the will is guided by a supreme principle of morality that he called the 'categorical imperative'. Kant viewed this imperative as the product of reason. So, the concept of justice is based on autonomy and his vision of justice is compatible with others autonomy. Kant's conception of right, autonomy, sovereignty, and his principle of justice is meant to regulate and safeguard individual's liberty and right on the basis of moral law that ought to be universalized.

The principle of freedom or autonomy will not conform to the principle of justice until its benefit or advantage is equally extended to each individual. The idea of autonomy is that "Autonomy of the will is that property of it by which it is a law to itself and it is independent of any property of the object of its volition"[27]. However, if it is defined as the absence of restraints, then autonomy cannot become the universal principle of justice until it is qualified by the principle of equality. It is clear that the restraint on autonomy of one does not become a threat to another's equal autonomy. Thus, the principle of equality becomes one of the necessary conditions in formulating a theory of justice.

In Kant's theory of justice, freedom of will or autonomy is the central concern. In order to understand Kant's conception of freedom and its implications for justice, it is essential to look at his metaphysics. In his metaphysical view, Kant makes the foundational distinction between noumenal freedom and phenomenal freedom. Kant makes a distinction between two different ways of knowing. The rst is the kind of knowing we can have of objects, or possible objects, as they appear or could appear to us. We can call this kind of knowledge that we gain from this way of knowing is phenomenal knowledge.The second way of knowing proposed by Kant is the knowing of things as they are in themselves. Kant calls this way of knowing as noumenal which designated intelligence, intellect or mind. For Kant, in contrast to phenomenal, knowledge of things as they are in themselves is inaccessible to humans. In Kant's view freedom exists in homo noumenon. In Kant's view, we can neither prove nor have certain knowledge that human beings possess free will. However, we can show that morality makes sense only if human beings are free. On this basis, we can reasonably postulate that human beings are free. And, on the basis of this postulate, we have the reason to comprehend extensively about the content of morality and justice. Through this understanding we can use reason to discover the laws of freedom, as Kant calls them, "laws that prescribe to us what ought to happen and what our duties are, as contrasted with laws of nature, which merely help us to explain what actually does happen in the world"[28].That's why we must assume that human beings have rationality and freedom. Both these attributes form the basis of all moral reasoning and in the absence of these, morality makes no sense. Kant's notion of justice is also based on the same dualism that underpins his entire metaphysics. Similarly, in Kant's thought, noumenon plays by far the larger role. The supersensible attributes of noumenon are the basis of Kant's theory of justice.

Kant's view on freedom is the backbone of his theory of justice. In order to understand this theory, therefore, it is important to grasp that Kant does not recommend the freedom can be a lack of constraints on one's actions. In fact, his concern for freedom as subjection to no other laws than those which a person gives to himself either alone or along with others. For him, to be free is not to lack constraints on one's actions, but to be independent of the constraints imposed by the arbitrary wills of others. Kant concluded that freedom so called autonomy of will is the supreme principle of morality and justice as well. Morality is possible only if the will is guided by a supreme principle of morality that is called the categorical imperative. This imperative as the product of reason and human beings as rational agents are autonomous self, have the capacity for moral self-government. For instance, they can set their own standards of conduct, as distinct from the demands made by their desires, and are able to decide and act on these standards.

Kant's notion of justice is surrounded with his entire moral theory postulates that man is known as *homonoumenon* is free. From this postulate, we can arrive at a single supreme principle of morality which he calls the categorical imperative. It is categorical in the sense that freedom applies to every individual irrespective of caste, colour, creed and sex. For Kant, freedom is a universal concept and it should be universally applied to every human being. Freedom is a necessary presupposition of all action as well as of all thinking. Freedom, however, is a complex concept throughout Kant's philosophy. Within Kant's moral theory, "there are two main types of freedom: inner and outer freedom"[29] Inner freedom is the primary subject of Kant's ethical theory while external freedom is the primary subject of Kant's theory of justice. External freedom in the most general sense is independence from constraints imposed by others but from normative perspective it is divide into two further categories; rightful external freedom which is freedom of action circumscribed by law of justice and lawless or wild external freedom which is the unrestricted anarchic liberty of the state of nature. The purpose of justice for Kant is to distinguish right from lawless external freedom and to determine what makes rightful freedom possible.

Kant's justice is based on rule of individual's liberty described by him as the principle of freedom of every member of a society as a human being. The purpose of this rule is to define an area of personal liberty within which individuals are free to act as they wish. For Kant, human beings are essentially choice making being. To be free as a human being is to possess freedom of choice. Now the principle of individual's liberty is a principle of justice and justice is concerned with external freedom. Therefore, the freedom of choice required by this principle must be external freedom of choice. In this way all members of a society are equally human in the sense that all share equally the same capacity for free choice. Hence, Kant clearly meant that external freedom of choice must be distributed equally among all individuals.

Kantian conception of justice has three essential characteristics, namely,

> First, Justice applies to only external relation between individuals in so far as their action may affect each other directly or indirectly. Secondly, it is not concerned with the wishes or desire of an individual but solely with the relationship of will to another person's will. Thirdly, it deals only with the form of the relations between the will in so far as they are regarded as free[30].

Synthesizing these three characteristics, Kant defines Justice as, "the aggregate of those conditions under which the will of one person can be conjoined with the will of another in accordance with a universal law of freedom"[31]. Kantian sense of justice is preoccupied with human being and for Kant human being as a rational being can become enlightened man if they come out from his immaturity by using his own reason securing the maximum set of liberty, equality, rights and autonomy that can be consistently enjoyed by all.

As I have already explained that freedom is the main concern for Kant's enlightenment and justice, now I will explain about his concept of right that also plays an important role in formulating enlightenment and justice in his theory. Kant says in the treatise *Rechtslehre*, "The only original right belonging to each man in virtue of his humanity is freedom…."[32]. "Every action is in accordance with right which enables the freedom of each man's will to assist side by side with the with the freedom of very other man, according to universal law"[33]. We can then suppose that when Kant develops freedom as the only original right of man and proposes to limit that freedom in the case of each individual solely by the demand for an equal freedom on the part of all the other individuals, it is evidently clear that for Kant an action would be contrary to right if it interferes with the formal freedom of one's neighbour. Justice presupposes equality of rights, of people and it is a kind of impartiality. It is a matter of securing the maximum set of equal rights that can be consistently enjoyed by all. Universal principle of rights of man in Kant's conception of justice is deduced from categorical imperative and it is the only principle that could be taken into account of Human Rights in terms of the constitution of a nation, state, ethnic, cultural and religious identities etc. Rights of man includes, right to life, liberty, property and pursuit of happiness and these rights were for Kant too the moral foundation of a just society. Thus, Kant view on rights of man is the most essential basis for the modern concept of human rights in which each individuals has a right to just treatment and reciprocal responsibility to ensure justice for others.

Justice demands that people should be treated equally as an end in themselves in terms of freedom and rights. This feeling would promote equality and justice, because the first duty of justice is to treat people impartially in the form of freedom and rights. As we have seen his sense of justice is a theory of the moral laws and so called laws of freedom that places limits on people's external actions and these limits can be coercively enforced. On the other hand, his basis of theory of justice is the universal principle of right, which is derived from the categorical imperative and which Kant formulates as follows that any action is just if it is compatible with everyone's freedom in accordance with a universal law. For Kant, the main concern of the principle of justice is to justify equal freedom and rights and the use of coercion to prevent people from hindering the freedom of others. The concern of justice is to secure freedom. It is certainly true according to the categorical principle that a coercive principle must not be compatible with everyone's freedom in accordance with a universal law.

Besides justice as a protection of freedom is the basic principle of his theory of justice, the universal principle of right is also one of the main concerns in formulating the principle of justice. Kant argued that "the rights of human beings are rooted in the original right to freedom, which belongs to every human being by virtue of his or her humanity"[34]. Justice consists in freedom of individual and each one should get equal freedom. Every human being as *homo noumena* is equal to each other because each possessed free will. He also argued that all human beings are inherently equal, in the sense that all are entitled not to be bound by others any more nor others can be bound by them. He asserts that all individuals of a state are entitled to being treated as equals by the laws, so that none should receive special privileges or be subject to unfavourable discrimination which entails injustice. He talks about two kinds of rights, public and private. Private right includes property, transactions, and contracts and other personal right such as the rights of parents over their children, rights of wife over husband and other's private right. On the other hand, public right has to do with the civil condition, that is, the state or civil society. The public right can be possible only in a civil society in which justice demands that its right should be equally recognized and enforced. In a just society, members of the civil society or the state reciprocally respect each other's freedom and rights by ceasing from violations of them by others. Kant argued that the rights of human beings are rooted in the original right to freedom, which belongs to every human being by virtue of his or her humanity.

Justice demands that everyone should be treated equally in terms of right, freedom, and autonomy. Therefore, we can say that human being as possessors of the capacity for freedom, are all equal. In Kant's notion of justice, the principle of justice ought to underpin equal freedom; rights for all persons regardless of any differences and it should be governed by the principle of reciprocity. In Kant's notion of justice, the principle of justice in the form of equal freedom of people who are superior in rank can always be identical in kind to the freedom of those who are their inferiors. In this way Kantian justice is also promotes equality in terms of freedom and public right.

Part - III

Justice and Social Contract

The social contract has been the dominant theory of justice in the western tradition of moral, social and political philosophy. Kant notes that justice protects individual autonomy and liberty, equality and right. Here, the question arises how should be protect individual's freedom and equality? For that, Kant has adopted the approach of social contract that is borrowed from some of his predecessors in early enlightenment including Thomas Hobbes, John Locke, and Jean-Jacques Rousseau. Kant, like Locke and Rousseau, believed that it is the institution or state that protects us from any kind of injustices. It is the institution which delivers impartial justice in the form of right, tolerance, autonomy and public and private reason. It is the social contract theory which sees principles of justice as the outcome of a contract people make for mutual advantage and to leave the state of nature to govern them by law. As we have seen, in contrast to the utilitarian view of justice, Kant placed the concept of freedom and right as reciprocity and the central principle of his theory of justice.

Kant's theory of justice regards the state as a man-made institution which delivers justice. Justice can be possible by the approach of social contract. Only autonomous and rational beings can enter into the social contact and make a common agreement in constructing the principle of absolute justice. Kant's status of justice is to protect individual freedom and rights. And for maintaining it social contract is a necessary tool because people's consent is necessary to evaluate whether the formulated principle is just or unjust for the sake of society. Therefore, in Kant's view, the approach of social contract is the prerequisite for the formulation of any principle for justice.

Kant takes this approach as a regulative principle to maintain justice within the society. Kant had employed the method of social contract in maintaining justice in society. Johnston, David says in his book: *A Brief History of Justice*,

> Public right by invoking the idea of the original contract to test and evaluate the public laws and policies. If it is plausible to suppose that the law or policy in question would have received the approval of all the members of a society in an original contract, then according to Kant, we must assume that that law or policy is just. If this supposition is implausible, then we may conclude that the law or policy is unjust[35].

Kantian justice can be delivered through contracterian approach where every sovereign and autonomous being makes an agreement about the principle of justice that acts only on that maxim through which you can at the same time will that it should become a universal law of justice.

It is believed that justice can bring only any by enter into a contract by autonomous individual to formulate the principle and laws which deliver justice.

> It is possible to maintain justice in relations among persons only by entering into the civil society that is by joining with others to form commonwealth (or state). He maintained that human beings are under an absolute duty to enter into that condition: a union as an end in itself which they all ought to share and which is thus an absolute and primary duty in all external relationships whatsoever among human beings ……. is only found in a society in so far as it constitutes a civil state, i.e. a commonwealth[36].

It is the state's function to safeguard and protect individual freedoms and equality and deliver justice to all human beings. Once enlightenment rationality makes people autonomous and sovereign they come to the general agreement of the principle of universality such as, treat human being as an end rather as means so that it can become the universal principle of justice for the dignity of human being.

Social Contract has been one of the best and dominant theories on authoritarian rule in the era of early enlightenment throughout the history. Each drew quite different viewpoint on the nature of political authority to deliver justice within social institutions. Now it is necessary to explain about social contract according to three thinkers. As we know that the divine theory of King was replaced by the consent theory which define in a simpler form that the citizen is tied to the governing authority to establish a just society. This consent theory is based on the hypothesis of a contract entered into by men living in the state of nature whereby political authority came into being. Thus, authority of the state is based on the consent of the people. The terms and condition of the contract were morally binding on those who made the agreement. Thus just political authority is based on the consent of the people. Hobbes says in *Leviathan,*

> the condition of man is a condition of war of every one against everyone, in which case everyone is governed by his own reason; and there is nothing he can make use of, that may not be a help

> unto him, in preserving his life against his enemies; it fallowed, that in such a condition, every man has a right to everything; even to one another's body. And therefore as long as this natural right of every man to everything endures, there can be no security to any man[37].

Hobbes's idea about social contract is that in a state of nature men lived in lawless and unjust society, not just because of things were not equally distributed but lack of rules and regulations.Human beings were able to move from the 'state of nature' to civil society because they are free to form a state with the support of their freedom and reason. Human beings established society through the people's consent to live together in harmony by creating common laws and a way to enforce them. People wanted a ruler of a sovereign or political body in order to be able to live in a civil society. Therefore, rational man overcomes the unjust state of nature to formulate the just society. Hobbes does not represent his social contract as generating principles of justice. He believed that justice

Locke offers a substantial theory of social contract and says that,

> In the 'state of nature', every man was equal. But there was no guarantee of individual rights. However, people live unsecure and unstable life, but they realize that they can enjoy their life if they can come together by means of contract. The purpose of contract is to form a civil society in which natural rights are guaranteed under a government established to enforce laws protecting natural right[38].

The journey from 'state of nature' to the social contract has been remarkable in establishing the civil society. The social contract guaranteed the formation of a just government to enforce laws for protecting natural right. The government (ruler) has the primary function of providing the conditions under which individuals can enjoy their natural rights. If the government is unable to provide a just condition under which people may enjoy their right then they are entitled to remove injustice.

The idea of social contract, however, took a highly philosophical form at the hands of Rousseau who reposed the fact of political obligation in the name of 'general will'. He says,

> The movement from the state of nature to the civil state produces a very remarkable change in man by substituting justice for instincts in his conduct, and giving his actions the morality they had formerly lacked. Then only when the voice of duty takes the place of impulses and appetites, does man, who so far had considered only himself, find that he is forced to act on different principles, and to consult his reason before listening to his inclinations[39].

Thus, after entering into a "civil society, man is no longer the slave of his mere impulses of appetite, he becomes the bound to obey the law of the general will which he prescribes to all including himself and that constitute his real liberty"[40].

Social contract is the method on which a civil society and its terms and condition have been formulated by an agreement among its members that determines the laws of their association. The fundamental question is that why do we need to institutionalise the principle of justice with the consent of all autonomous being. However, there have been disagreements among philosophers to implement social contract to establish civil society or state or any institution as a necessary tool to deliver justice.

Hegel strongly opposed to social contract approach because it has no historical foundation. "Social contract theory could be explanatory as an ethical and logical advanced to provide a moral evaluation and reconstruction of constitution to justify an evaluation. But it certainly has no historical evidence"[41]. Hegel was anti-contracterian because he had a different understanding of the relationship between the individual and the civil society. He believes, "since the state is Geist objectified, it is only as one of its members that the individual himself has objectivity, genuine individuality, and an ethical life"[42]. It is the individual's membership of the state that makes him spiritual and concrete universal. Hegel's chief criticism to the notion of the social contract is that,

> It operates with an abstract, a cultural and non-contextual view of man. That is to say that the idea of social contract has cogency only because it assumes that the individual (the outer), so that from this putative separateness, membership of the state can be optional and a matter of voluntary choice. This means that the state's existence now depends on the individual's capricious will through his individuality given consent[43].

Hegel regarded Geist as the centre of the state. Since Geist is rational and the basic feature of rationality is its universality, therefore, the laws of the state should be known to all.

As a matter of fact it was the social contract method that was rejected by David Hume who also rejected it both on its historical and philosophical grounds. Hume is not a contractarian; his account of justice, based on convention. As Nussbaum says in "Social Contracts and Three Unsolved Problems of justice" in book *Frontiers of Justice*, "Like the contracterians, Hume relies on mutual advantage as the key to the emergence and maintenance of justice"[44]. The rule of justice depends on the particular state and conditions in which men are placed. For instance, the sense of justice will bring when the condition is moderate in wealth and possessions. Once the rules of justice are framed and people see the usefulness of the rule that provide justice to all. That's why for Hume, justice is convention whose usefulness is directly proportional to the situation and circumstances wherein people are placed.

> Government for Hume is not always necessary nor is it possible for primitive societies to live without consent of the governed, neither are all men created free and equal. In the same way the foundations of government and the reason for its sovereignty and stability rest upon a far broader basis in the human nature than the simplest consent of the governed[45].

As C.J. Berry writes,

> History reveals the uniform principles and regular springs of human nature and historical knowledge is only possible because of the constancy implicit in human action. Thus, despite that there is no record of the origin of government; nevertheless … that we

> can trace it plainly in the nature of man. Given what we know about the various but contingent conditions of social life, reasonably conjecture is permissible, similarly the philosophical argument. Utilising the distinction between natural and artificial virtues, only worked in its required may because it consists of universal proposition[46].

It is clear from the above statement that, to maintain justice in the state we did not need to enter into the social contract to form a government. The authority of government is derived (for all practical intents and purposes) from force, custom and historic continuity and the disapprobation or disapproval aroused by the attempt to subvert or overthrow by force any system of authority standing for law and order.

Throughthe criticism of social contract by Hume, Kant uses this method as a regulative principle because it helps us to organise our social affairs.

Kant writes in *Perpetual Peace,*

> In this civil union, self-sought, yet sought reluctantly, man is able to turn his most unlovable equalities to a profitable use. They bind this society together. They are the instruments by which he wins for himself self-culture. It is here with men as it is with the trees in a forest: just because each one strives to deprive the other of air and sun, they compel each other to seek both above, and thus they grow beautiful and straight. Whereas those that, in freedom and isolation from one another, shoot out their branches and at will, grow stunted and crooked and awry[47].

The social contract is advantageous to all people who join the contract to unite into a common principle that binds all human beings. In Kant's contract, each individual in contract is free, equal, and independent. Though everyone is free and autonomous in social contract, still they come together to form a community in order to get equal social opportunity in maintaining justice. This is the mutual advantage of the contract which provides sufficient motive for entering into it.

The social contract is such an idea,

> ...we by no mean hold that this contract.....actually exists as a fact for it cannot possibly be so..... it is merely an idea of reason which nonetheless has undoubted practical reality for it can oblige legislator to frame this laws in such a way that they could have been produced by the united will of a whole nation and to regard each subject.....as if he had consented within the general will. This is the test of the rightfulness of every public law[48].

Unlike social contract of Rousseau in the form of the general will, it is neither the will of the majority, nor the will of the political entity but the will of all that unites under the social contract. Its criteria of legitimacy is that a one sided people can be free and yet be subject to social regulation, Kant's use of public reason brought common agreement and its legitimacy based on each and everyone's consent. In Kant's philosophy, social contract is formulated on the basis of public reason which promotes individual's active consents to a government.

Kant says in *Rechtslehre,* about the insight of social contract and why he has formulated social contract theory. Kant asserts that, "morality consists in the set of rules governing behaviour that rational people would accept, on the condition that others accept them as well"[49]. Kantian social agreement brings out from the morality that we ought to make an agreement so that it delivers impartial justice to all human beings. A just society ought to be based on a fair system of cooperation among free and autonomous beings and the function of social contract is to protect individual freedom and equality among all human beings. His entire theory of justice is based on principle consent of practical reason of enlightened being who makes a common principle for the welfare of a perfectly just society.He emphasizes that the individuals in the original contract are rational in the sense that they prefer to become members of a society whom they represent to obtain a greater rather than a lesser share of the beneûts of social cooperation. The fact that the individuals are rational does not entail that they as the members of a society whom they represent are egoistic. Those members may, for example, wish to use a portion of their shares to promote causes that benet others. He also emphasizes that the enlightened individuals are reasonable. They understand that they must be willing to reach to agreement with their counterparts on fair terms.

It is the enlightenment tradition which gives the status of justice to all, based on the social contract. It is the view that person's moral and political obligations are dependent upon a contract or agreement among them to form the society in which they live. In the beginning the social contract theory of the state implies that there was a time when men lived without any recognised civil law or without the state. That's why Hobbes advocated justice in absolute monarchy. Unlike Hobbes, Locke's status of justice advocated in the form of natural rights, and Rousseau's justice advocated in a collective sovereignty in the name of the general will and principle of generality. Kant's social contract adopted the freedom to use of public reason in terms of public right. The social contract is an approach intended to explain the appropriate relationship between individuals and the society and their terms and conditions of the institution. Social contract asserts that individuals unite into political societies by a process of mutual consent, agreeing to abide by common rules and accept corresponding duties to protect themselves and others from any kind of injustices, violence and other kinds of harm. It is one of the vehicles in the civil society which promotes justice.

Kant's theory of justice is regulated and governed with the help of social contract. The idea of the public right includes the right to enter into social contract through common principle, that is, the principle of public reason, and public reason like natural right of Locke, and general will of Rousseau, is the main pillar of social contract. The public use of reason is not the reason of the political organism but it is the reason of public to adopt the method of social contract to maintain justice if their freedom, right, autonomy would be in threat.

Generally, Social contract implies that every autonomous individual in the society is represented by an end in itself in the kingdom of end in which the rational being come together to reach an agreement (ought to treat humanity as an end rather as a means so that it can become universal principle of justice) that will shape the principle or laws in commonwealth. The method of social contract is to imagine that a commonwealth or civil society must be founded by an agreement among its members that determines the terms of their association.

> Kant had employed this method in his theory of public right by invoking the idea of the original contract to test the justice of public laws and policies. If it is plausible to suppose that the law or policy in question would have received the approval of all the members of a society in an original contract, then according to Kant we must assume that that law or policy is just. If this supposition is implausible, then we may conclude that the law or policy is unjust[50].

Social contract is the parameter to assess whether policy is just or unjust. "For Kant, the idea of the original contract is the vehicle for determining whether or not laws and policies are just, much as the categorical imperative is the test for ascertaining whether or not individuals' maxims and discrete actions are rightful"[51]. The approach of social contract helps to assess whether the laws and policies are just or not. The maxims of categorical imperative evaluate whether an individual's action is right or not. Kant's conception of justice is an ideal theory of justice and its principle must be framed for a perfectly just society. We can say that it can be possible to maintain justice in relations among persons only by entering into the civil society by joining with others in a commonwealth or state. He maintained that human beings are under an absolute duty to enter into that condition of civil society: "a union as an end in itself which they all ought to share and which is thus an absolute and primary duty in all external relationships whatsoever among human beings is only found in a society in so far as it constitutes a civil state, i.e. a commonwealth"[52]. Here, Kant's main argument is that only by constituting a collective will or so called public right we enter into a civil state and it is backed by coercive power can assure people that others will respect their rights. Before the creation of such a power each person possesses the right to do what seems right and good to that person. However, in this pre-political condition each person is also exposed to the possibility of being constrained by the arbitrary will of others which leads to injustice. Justice requires protection of individual freedom and equality, and what people must do is to join with others to create a state that possesses sufcient power to enforce the rights of its citizens. The only possible kind of just society is a just state which safeguards individual freedom and right. A just state is the product of an original contract agreed upon by those who become members of that state. For Kant, this contract is an idea of reason rather than an empirical or historical fact. As a matter of justice, the subjects of a state owe absolute obedience to its sovereign. His concern is that there can be no justice without a state and any rebellion to a state constitutes a threat to its very existence and hence a threat to justice. We can make a just society by the civil condition or the principle of social norms and laws, because these norms are the product formulated by the autonomous and sovereign being and in Rousseau's terms of general will agreed upon by those autonomous being. For Kant, this contract and agreement brings out from the use of public reason or idea of rationality rather than any historical fact. In Kant's view, a just society is one whose principal goal is to maintain social relations of mutual respect and toleration among free and equal citizens. Its purpose is not to enhance their material welfare but overall welfare. Kant opened up a new territory for thinking about justice.

To bring this chapter to an end, we can say that the principle conclusion of the theory of.

Notes

1. Kant, *Enlightenment East and West*. p. 3.
2. Michael J Sandel, *Liberalism and the Limits of Justice*. p. 15.
3. Johnston David, "Kant's theory of Justice," p. 142.
4. *Ibid.,* p. 22.
5. *Ibid.,* p. 145.
6. *Ibid.,* p. 144.
7. *Ibid.,* p. 144.
8. Kamenka, Eugene. "What is justice?". p. 21.
9. Michael, J Sandel, *Liberalism and the Limits of Justice.* p. 6.
10. *Ibid.,* p. 2.
11. Kant. *Critique of Practical Reason*. p. 30.
12. Kant, *The Moral Law: Ground Work of Metaphysic of Morals*. p. 31.

13. Onarao'Neill, *Constructions of Reason: Explorations of Kant's Practical Philosophy*. pp. 2013-14.
14. *Ibid.*, p. 214.
15. *Ibid.*, p. 22.
16. Kant, *Ground of Metaphysic of Morals*. p. 29.
17. Johnston, David. "Kant's Theory of Justice," p. 164.
18. *Ibid.*, p. 136.
19. Kant, *Groundwork of Metaphysic of Morals*. p. 101.
20. *Ibid.*, p. 33.
21. *Ibid.*, p. 34.
22. Kant, *Practical Philosophy*, p. 99.
23. Kant, *The Moral Law: Kant's Groundwork of Metaphysics of Morals*. p. 104.
24. *Ibid.*, p. 39.
25. Kant, *Ground of Metaphysic of Morals*. p. 45.
26. *Ibid.*, p. 45.
27. Johnston, David, "Kant's Theory of Justice," p. 148.
28. Kant, *Doctrine of Virtue*. p. 213
29. Allen D Rosen. *Kant's Theory of Justice*. p. 75.
30. *Ibid.*, p. 75.
31. Kant, *Rechtslehre Einleitung*, p. 40.
32. *Ibid.*, p. 78.
33. Kant, *Science of Right*, p. 6.
34. David, "Kant's theory of Justice," p. 210.
35. *Ibid.*, p. 160-61.
36. Hobbes, *Leviathan*. p. 91.
37. Locke, *The Second Treatise of Government*. p. 52.
38. Rousseau, *The Social Contract*. p. 46.
39. *Ibid.*, pp. 46-48.
40. Singh.*Freedom and Causation with Special Reference to Hegel's Overcoming of Kant*. p. 102.
41. *Ibid.*, p. 103.
42. *Ibid.*, p. 103.
43. Nussbaum, "Social Contracts and Three Unsolved Problems of justice", p. 46.
44. Singh.*Freedom and Causation with Special Reference to Hegel's Overcoming of Kant*. p. 104.
45. Christopher, J Berry. *Hegel and Human Nature*. p. 164.

46. Kant, *Perpetual Peace: A Philosophical Essay.* p. 54.
47. Kant, *Theories and Praxis in Kant's Political Writing*. p. 177.
48. Kant, *Rechtslehre Einleitung*. p. 145.
49. Johnston, David. "Kant's Theory of Justice", p. 210.
50. *Ibid.,* p. 164.
51. *Ibid.,* p. 161.

Conclusion

Justice is considered as one of the important virtue along with wisdom, courage and temperance. Moreover, people who possess the virtue of justice would be able to exist with other fellow beings in the society justly, and peacefully. The good life is thought to be the kind of life that persons ought to seek. A common approach to defining the good life in these ancient works is to work out an analysis and description of human nature and then to construct a model of human life that would fulfill this nature, one to which some or all persons were capable of conforming. Amongst the Greeks, for Aristotle, the ultimate goal of human is the pursuit of happiness or *eudaimonia. Eudaimonia* is realized in activity in which a person is to seek over the course of a complete life. It is a specification of what it is to live well as a human being. In his view, it is only through daily practice of both the intellectual and the moral virtues over the course of a complete lifetime that one can achieve eudaimonia. It is through the activities of human goodness that we can achieve it. Living a life in accordance with virtue is usually taken to be necessary for eudaimonia, because virtue is at least partially constitutive of eudaimonia. Aristotle also acknowledges still further basic requirements for achieving eudaimonia. For example, material wealth, which provides physical comfort and security, is necessary to free the individual to pursue the good life.

The framing project of Aristotle is to identify the highest good, the end we should aim at for its own sake and not for the sake of anything further. Aristotle seems to find it obvious that well-being is the sole ultimate good, the only condition worth pursuing for its own sake. Aristotle finds that the highest human good consists in "activity of soul in conformity with excellence [*arete*], and if there are more than one excellence, inconformity with the best and most complete." Thus, the focus shifts here once more, this time from *eudaimonia* to *arete*, from well-being to excellence. For Aristotle, a thing's excellence is conceptually connected to its function and thereby to its welfare. Aristotle says,

"There remains, then, an active life of the element that has a rational principle ... ; and as this too can be taken in two ways,rational principle ... ; we must state that life in the sense of activity is what we mean;for this seems to be the more proper sense of the term. Now if the function of man is an activity of soul in accordance with, or not without, rational principle, and if we say that a so-and-so and a good so-and-so have a function which is the same in kind, . . .human good turns out to be activity of soul in conformity with excellence."

Although it is usual to render eudaimonia into English as 'happiness', the Greek term actually corresponds much more closely to our notion of well-being: a complete state of being and doing well. Well-being concern the prudential value of a life, namely, how well it is going for the individual whose life it is. It is the idea that the person lives a good life when the person manages to get what he or she wants. It addresses the problem of how to generate and allocate productive resources to achieve the best social state where justice is understood as a quality of exhibiting enlightened and moral excellence of persons and affairs. It concern why should I be just? What ought I to do or not to do for my enlightenment or my ignorance? Is hatred can be fight with compassion or discrimination with recognition and respect? How can we remove the chain of sufferings and reaches at the stage of enlightenment? Is the path of enlightenment and morality going to ensure justice? In order to address these questions, the book- ***Justice as Enlightenment and Morality*** focuses on the ethical dimension of justice which begins and ends with human being whereby a 'just man' connotes not only that he/she ought to be good in the social sense, but most importantly be good to his/her self, which is an 'enlighten and moral awakening' so that one can attain individual happiness and happiness of the society.

Justice is indeed a philosophical contested concept. Kant's contribution lies in formulating justice in terms of absolute, perfect and ideal which could be presupposed in making any judgement on justice. This concept of justice was in the process of evolving for a long time, perhaps very long time. I can say that the social contract of early enlightenment; enlightenment rationality and morality have been the most operative term in formulating the Kant's notion of absolute justice. Early Enlightenment thinkers tried to establishes a just or equal society through the method of social contract and to maintain individual rights, equality, toleration, and general will.

Among the early enlightenment thinkers we have Thomas Hobbes, John Locke and Jean- Jacques Rousseau who adopted the method of social contract to repudiate feudal monarchy and aristocracy. They used the natural right that is freedom to enter into civil society to protect their natural rights especially right to life, liberty and property. Hence, the provision of human rights or natural rights is automatically linked with the concept of toleration to make a just society. In this way justice consist in the protection of human rights, sense of toleration, and respect for others rights and freedom to enter into contract.

At the time of pre-enlightenment the society was having a justice based on the rights and privileges which were found in the hands of very few people, *not all*. It was Locke who brought the concept of justice in the form of natural rights. He regarded that people should have natural right to enter into social agreement to establish institutions. This is meant to repudiate monarch's divine right and to develop a just society which gives human rights, toleration, equality, fraternity to every individual. Locke's notion of justice emerged in the struggle against monarchy and hereditary privileges with the help of social contract. He attempted to create an institution such as civil society or states which could provide justice in the form of equal rights for all. So justice in Locke is based on the institutional approach rather than authoritarian regime of king. This kind of justice as an institution tries to remove discrimination among human beings on the ground of individual's caste, creed, sex, race, and treats them with equal dignity and moral worth of all being. The function of justice in enlightenment is to regulate the mutual toleration between individuals and groups with social contract. Here the quest of justice should aim at evolving reasonable rules on human rights, toleration and it should be applied impartially to all.The core commitments of Locke's notion of justice are: firstly, justice consists of applying general rules impartially to all citizens regardless of their circumstances or differences for natural right. Secondly, justice in the principle of constitutionalism that is the concept of justice exists in constitution or rules of law. Justice is opposed to rule by a dictator's rule. Thirdly, justice entails about basic individual rights, such as right to life, liberty, property, freedom of religion, freedom of expression and freedom association and so on so.

In early enlightenment it was the liberalists who brought sense of justice in the society especially Locke and Rousseau. They employed the concept of the social contract theories to share a set of core principles and assumptions that include the principle of human equality, individualism, autonomy and toleration. They claim that each human being is an equal and autonomous individual and no person has a natural authority to over another. They appeal to the principle of voluntarism in explaining the origin of moral and political obligations and to the principle of consent in explaining how the autonomous individual voluntarily renounces her natural liberty to the state, thereby acquiring moral and political obligations for making a just society. Locke have made a significant contribution to repudiate king's special power and emphasised on the individual's right, toleration, social contract to move from unjust society to just society.

Rousseau's status of justice is based on the principle of generality and in his description of the general will in the social contract. Rousseau's general will give us insight to formulate the principle of justice which establishes equality among the citizens in that they all pledge themselves under the same conditions and must all enjoy the same rights. Hence by the act of the general will binds all the citizens equally so that the sovereign recognise the whole body of the nation and makes no distinction and discrimination between any of the members who compose it. The conception of justice consists in generality, commonality, impartiality, universality, equality of all citizens. As we know that, the status of justice in the general will is perfectly general with respect to any given political community. It is based on general both in the sense that it reflects the general welfare of the whole community, and it is general with respect to each member who has contributed to making just society. Rousseau's general will provides us to formulate the principle of justice. These are namely: first is the condition and foundation of justice is based on the principle of generality which refers to the general interest. Second is that it relates to public good of the entire community and general laws take into account the well-being of the whole political community and not just its largest or most influential parts. Third, it consists of applying general rules impartially to all man regardless of their circumstances and differences. Fourth, it is based on the principle of generality which requires laws to be abstract and indifferent to the particular identities of the persons making them as well as those to whom they will apply and it can bring when man acts in the state against his own will under the direction of the general will.

Rousseau's view of justice lies in general will and its basis is the social contract, equitable one, common to all, it can have no end but the common good. Rousseau's conception of justice implies at once generality, commonality. Status of justice is general with respect to the whole political community and social institution. It is impartiality and universality in the sense general as opposed to merely partial or interested. It is also equality and uniformity of applying generally to all members of the political community equally and in precisely the same way irrespective of their differences. It is an active political willing made by the whole people, not for them, regardless of the substance of the law, and generalizability means the justice of a law is confirmed by whether we would accept its consequences for ourselves and others as a more general rule. Though justice in the general will by means of the just and proper rules with respect to all members of the political community reflecting either what they actually do desire, or as is more likely, what they should desire if they were aware of their truly general interests. The principle of generality helps us to formulate the laws of any social institutions and political community. In his conception laws and justice are complementary and supplementary to each other. For instance, laws of any institution provide us the basis and foundation for making the just society. Thus the concept of general will provides an impartial law which is the backbone of the modern procedural view of justice in Rousseau. This is what I have discussed in the first chapter of the dissertation.

Although Locke and Rousseau advocated a view justice which consisted in the protection and preservation of natural right and establish on the basis of general will in the form of social contract, yet their conception of justice was not universally applicable and could not give complete insight of absolute justice. Though they have applied the social contract to formulate the principle of justice but this principle somehow could not formulate the principle of morality that universally bind to all human being into one law that is called categorical imperative, i.e. the universal law of morality. It is Kant's absolute justice, morality gives us some insight into *how* justice ought to be and not what is to be just.

In fact Kant's enlightenment rationality gives us insight of absolute justice to become enlightened by overcoming immaturity and self-incurred habit by using one's own understanding. For him absolute justice can possible if everyone can become enlightened and act in such a way so that can be a principle of justice. In Kant's justice enlightened individual can enter into a social contract to formulate the principle of justice that ought to be implemented by everyone.

I have developed Kant's absolute justice with the help of enlightenment rationality, morality and social contract. Kant's enlightenment rationality offers the best way to repudiate mentor or authority in thinking, willing and feeling. It helps us to become autonomous and sovereign to use right, tolerance, freedom and public and private reason.

According to Kant anyone can become enlightened if s/he can live with rational and moral principle. Enlightenment claims that progress is possible through the use of reason and the spread of enlightenment and humanity is summed up in Kant's dictum "Have courage to use your own reason"[1]. Reason alone can enlightened humanity from the, tradition, custom, and inherited authority and allow them to realize freedom by submitting it their own conscious purposes or we can say that "*sapereaude*or have courage to use your own understanding to become just man"[2]. The enlightenment rationality is the ultimate outcome of just man by giving right, tolerance, autonomy, equality, fraternity, justice, public and private reason. It focuses that human beings are free to make and transform themselves accordance with their own critical rationality.

In one aspect enlightenment rationality helps us to become just man by using their one's own right; the other aspect is morality is also justifying the sense of absolute justice. It is the morality which taught us to be moral under all circumstances so that their action becomes the universal law of morality. So that once person become enlightened can formulate the universal principle of morality which gives some insight of justice. In chapter II, I have discussed in details all these issues.

The purpose of this dissertation is to explicate the Kant's insight of the image of just man for entire humanity to make them sovereign and autonomous being. The majority work of this dissertation is dedicated to explicate and develop the image of just and enlightened being so that they act freely and formulate the universal principle of morality that ought to become the principle of justice.

In Kant's notion of justice, concept of enlightenment, rationality and freedom plays an important role to makes public use of one's own reason in all matters. As enlightenment come up with maturity and freedom to use one's own public reason from immaturity and irrational behaviour guided by others in the form of authority, tradition and customs play an important role in formulating the notion of justice. It is enlightenment rationality brought a great change on society, such as freedom, equality, fraternity and justice by emphasising on equal freedom, universal right, tolerant for others right, autonomy, public and private reason to every man being a rational. It provides a vision of just society wherein every man gets universal and equal treatment in terms of freedom and right for social and political action to become the enlightened man. There are various enlightenment ingredients which helps us to become just, autonomous, and sovereign being. These are rights, tolerance, and autonomy, public and private reason. Right is one of the important contributors to make individual autonomous and sovereign. However, there have been a certain attempts to discuss rights in terms of the constitution of nation, ethnic, and religious identities, etc. but to define universal and human right in the most general sense then Kant's categorical imperative is the only principle that shapes the Universal Human Rights. As maxims of categorical imperative cannot be strange to any culture and helps to have universal insight of justice.

Kant's enlightenment emphasised on the virtue of independence which is the basic principle of right to become autonomous. To create enlightened age for just man we need to requires right and independence in the form of free will to set her own purposes and not treating herself instead either as a means to be used in pursuit of another person's purposes. The interference with another person's freedom creates a form of dependence which becomes barrier in the way of enlightenment. Kant's conception of right in enlightenment guarantees equal freedom to utilise their right and make sure that no person be subject to the choice of another. In this way the habit of independence give the insight of the image of just man who can be autonomous or independence in their freedom to use their right properly.

Once the person becomes autonomous and sovereign which automatically creates the habit of tolerance for others right. It inculcates the reciprocal attitude toward others right, autonomy, freedom and especially to respect others who have different opinions, religious belief, race and practices. Thus, Kantian conception of tolerance helps us to become just man by inculcating the habit of tolerance to live peacefully by accepting others dignity, right and autonomy. It is the only virtue that promotes justice to live to get along with others. It is the tolerance which makes social justice by tolerating and giving respects to others right and freedom so that everyone irrespective of cast, creed, sex, and religion coexist and live peacefully and just fully. Here I would say only enlightened person can tolerate and willingly accept the general principle that binds all in a pluralist global society.

In enlightenment rationality and its idea of autonomy play an important role because it encourages us to think rationally of any decision making. For Kant, it is our duty of every one to have courage to use freedom, right and decision making under the self-legislative law so that it becomes universalise. The concept of autonomy will provide an alternative perspective on the most vital question of how to choose one's mode of living to become just toward himself and society also.

Enlightenment rationality leads individual to become autonomous and intellectual independence in public and private reason which automatically helps to acquire the image of just man. It is the duty of every person use their public reason freely and it should not restrict by anyone in the form of authority anyone else otherwise Kant's dream of enlightenment and the idea of just man would be unachievable. Therefore public reason is ought to be independence from any authority and shouldn't be restricted but the private reasons can be restricted to some extent by the authority. Public reason is the only way to think for the betterment of the society.

Therefore, we can say that autonomous and sovereign person can fallow the dream of Kant's enlightenment rationality: "*Sapereaude": Think boldly, take courage, and use your own understanding"*[3] to serve the purpose of right, tolerance, autonomy, public and private reason. It is enlightenment makes the people to become autonomous so that they choose a maxim which can become universal law of morality. The sense of justice in Kant is self- imposed that is law of justice is democratically self-imposed. Now the question arises why we need justice? The sense of justice requires because it protect and safeguard our freedom, right and equality.

Kant's absolute kind of justice bring out from his moral principle such as universality, end-in-itself and kingdom of end. Kant's justice as an,

> act externally so that free exercise of your personal will could be brought under general law together with the freedom of everyone- consummates the separation between law and justice on the one hand as concerned only with external behaviour, morality on the other hand as concerned with inner life[4]

In Kant's notion of justice morality is the foundation on which his sense of justice evolved. In Kant's view the principle of justice evolved out of moral principle. So we can say that justice and morality are inseparable from each other and in fact both are the two sides of same coin, one is based on external life other is based on inner life. It is the morality which evaluates our inner action either it is just or unjust, while justice controlled external action with others in terms of freedom, right, toleration, autonomy, public and private reason. In Kant's view, justice is a moral concept which treats every person equally that is according to general principle or rule which binds all rational beings into one principle is called categorical imperative.

Kant's moral principle such as universality, end-in-itself and kingdom of end give insight of justice that how it ought to be? What is to be just action? Moral action is what if I do, would be good for everybody to do. It is the universality tells us that we ought only to do that act which we can will to be a universal law. It shows that every principle of justice should be deduced from general law so that it can impose to everyone under all circumstances. There should be no occasion under which an exception of injustice is made. For instance human right should be universally implemented and there should not be any kind of discrimination.

The moral law requires us always to treat others as an end in itself. Through this principle, we can formulate sense of justice for humanity is based on the principle of end-in-itself. It gives universal justice for the dignity and respect for humanity. We ought to be just in treating human being and it shows in the principle that "Act in such a way that you always treat humanity, whether in your own person or in the person of any other, never simply as a means but always at the same time as an end."[5] It shows that, it is just to treat humanity as an end rather means. Justice demands that people should be treated equally as an end in themselves.

This is one of the important principles of morality that gives insight for social justice in the formula of the kingdom of ends such as – "so act as if you were through your maxims a law making member of a kingdom of an ends"[6]. It shows that, act in that way so that your maxims would harmonize with a kingdom of ends. It is life world of different rational being under common and universal laws. Through this common life world and its principle can bring harmony between the maxim of universal law and end-in-itself.in the society instead of some differences.

In Kant's Justice is an absolute notion and it ought to be universally implemented on autonomy that everyone's freedom should act in that way so that it becomes the universal law of justice. Justice consists if free will of one person can act according to the universal law of autonomy which coexists with one free will to the others to reach to the universal principle of autonomy and liberty.

We can say that Kant's Good will is one of the foundational pillars because it provides a vision for absolute justice that *how* justice ought to be. It will inculcate once individual act on the maxim of categorical imperative. This is the one principle on which a will can never be unjust and inconsistent with itself and always impartial and just because it is compatible with universal principle of justice.

It is moral obligation to adopt perfect and imperfect duty, to acquire the nature of good will. For instance, anyone can acquire the virtue of good will once he or she will fallow the maxim of morality namely universality and end in itself. It gives the idea that how to formulate a maxim that can bring justice. Good will develops the idea that justice is self-imposed i.e. law of justice is democratically self-imposed. As we know that autonomy is good if it use in justified ways. It can also be unjust for example an enlightened person cannot act on the maxim of universality and end in itself. Kant argues that only one thing is good in and of itself unconditionally, which is a 'good will' which implies that the will of a person who wants to do just action. A will can become just if it act from the sense of duty and no other motives and inclination. Right and autonomy can be just. If it is used by good will otherwise it can be misused by bad will.

It helps that how to use enlightenment concepts such as right, tolerance, autonomy, and freedom to use of public and private reason to acquire the image of just and moral man. In this way enlightened and moral person can construct a good will in formulating a universal principle which promotes peace and justice in the society.

Kant's principle of absolute justice formulated with the help of enlightenment and morality that states autonomous being can act on the basis of universal law and it has to be maintained that their action is always to be considered as an end and never simply as means because every enlightened being exist as an end in itself not merely as a means for arbitrary use of will whether for himself and for others.

Now the question of justice when we need arises, only where there is a conflict of action and interest. In real life people disagree on universal moral principle namely: universality, end in itself and kingdom of end because they have conflicting interests. On the other hand if we put them on a where this conflicting interest cannot influence them, then, they can automatically reach to the agreement. When it is supposed that people are disinterested and not willing to act in that way so that it can become universal law of autonomy, humanity as an end rather means, and kingdom of end in case then there the question of justice arise. In Kant's justice people can make contract to formulate the principle of justice that is betterment for him and for the entire society. For instance universal law of freedom, autonomy, liberty, equality, right, and toleration, public and private reason to make a society more just like kingdom of end in Kant's thought.

The sole purpose to use social contract in the Kant's justice is to formulae just principle in society in which right, autonomy, toleration, public and private use of reason, human dignity and equality are guaranteed under a government to enforce laws protecting right and concerning their disputes. Kant's sense of justice is regulated and governed with the help of social contract. The idea of the public right includes the right to enter into social contract through common use that is the use of public reason. The public use of reason is not the reason of the political organism but it is the reason of public to adopt the method of social contract to maintain justice if their freedom, right, autonomy would be in threat.

Kant's theory of justice aims to maintain social relation of mutual respect, human dignity, tolerance, right and reciprocity among free and equal individuals in the society. It is the social contract of enlightened being to come together and make principle that constitutes the foundation of absolute justice in a perfectly just society. These are: Justice ought to be under the universal principle of autonomy of will so that everyone should act on maxim of morality then it can become the principle of law and that can be justified by the moral law of categorical imperative.The other principle of justice consists in the concept of enlightenment and morality. These are:The Enlightenment Rationality states that human oriented concept such as rights, autonomy, tolerance, public and private use of reason should be categorically implemented within the society. So that everyone in the society can acquire the image of just man.

Justice lies in the principle of morality because it helps us to evaluate the notion of justice and formulate the universal principle of justice that ought to be universalized under all circumstances. The sense of justice consists in the moral principle for instance, treating humanity as end not as a means provides us a sense of justice to treat human being as a moral worth and dignity. Kant had formulated the universal principles of morality that give us insight for maintaining absolute justice so that it ought to be universalised. This is what I have developed in chapter III.

Today, human being are facing various kinds of suffering, ill treatment towards each other, and impartiality among fellow-beings in the family and exploitation of human being in the society which will lead to the destruction of humankind. In order to address these problems, Western approach of Kantian enlightenment and Eastern approach of Buddhist enlightenment is the need of an hour. Although, European enlightenment emphasises on the importance of reason over authority and Buddhist enlightenment concerned about transformative awakening which focuses on the ultimate goal of achieving nirvana which considered to be a release from endless cycle of suffering and rebirth.

Kant has rightly pointed out that, enlightenment means thinking for oneself which involves thinking and thus following the dictates of reason. I would say that. thinking is itself rule governed and thinking for oneself as opposed to deferring to others As a result, thinking for oneself involves believing on the basis of rational norms and reasons. It is the reason free ourselves from our emotions of jealousy, anger, hatred and selfishness otherwise these emotions disturb our inner self and make us less mindful and subsequently harm both oneself and others. It is in this sense, I have argued that transforming one's moral orientation is very important. Since, morality helps us to overcome the afflictive emotions and transform oneself in a just manner. The enlightenment encourages us to transform one's orientation from selflove to recognition of and respect for our common humanity.

Kant's theory of justice is to maintain social relation of mutual respect, human dignity, tolerance, right and reciprocity among free and equal individual in the global society. The principles of justice constructed with a common and moral obligation in society. Certainly Kant's absolute justice will fill the gap between various debates on moral, legal, religions and human right issues throughout history.

The idea of 'justice as enlightenment and morality' is the key to awakening is the realization of the fundamental interdependence and interconnectedness of human beings. Moreover, the interconnectedness of all existence underlies in our fundamental equality which rooted in our common susceptibility to suffering. In order to overcome partiality requires retraining the mind through meditative practice, which leads to a transformation of consciousness, which includes a more mindful awareness of interdependence and not in our autonomy and capacity to reason. It may point out that, rational insight alone is not enough to achieve a systematic reorientation of one's thinking and action. Since, selfishness, anger, and hatred are rooted in our egocentric orientation and mere enlightenment approach of reason cannot overcome these passions. More importantly, human wisdom or reason alone is not enough; they also need to retrain the habits of the mind through moral practice, and perhaps also years of meditative practice. It is the process of enlightenment making human being progressively selfdirected in thought and action through the awakening of one's intellectual powers, leads ultimately to a better, more fulfilled human existence.

In other words, enlightenment requires increased wisdom, moral restraint and meditation which underlies in the eightfold path of Buddhism. It is the heart of the middle path which turns from extreme and encourages us to seek simple approach on the basis of right understanding, right thought, right speech, right action, right livelihood, right effort, right mindfulness and right concentration. It is like Kant's categorical imperative which commands, those who have justice in mind will never have partiality in dealing with other people through their physical, verbal and mental actions. Because this kind of impartiality is to be taken as the golden rule for all religions, which is understood in the like manner that we shall not do any injustice to others in the way that we do not want others do the same injustice unto us. In this way, the concepts of justice are known as 'Ethical Dhammas', the foundation of which is the 'Eightfold Noble Path' as the Middle Way in Buddhism. People, who possess the afore-mentioned virtues, would be able to ex-exist with other fellow-beings in the society, justly, peacefully and honestly.

Therefore, the enlightened person rejects the principle of self - love and embraces and internalizes the authority of morality and moral conviction that awakening one's mind to inculcate the virtue of love, kindness and compassion. They will avoid from the following types of prejudices; firstly, prejudice caused by love, second prejudice caused by hatred, third prejudice caused by delusion and fourth prejudice caused by fear in order to lead to a better, more satisfying life. In this way, justice as enlightenment and morality very well fits in the debate between 'what is justice' and 'what ought to be just' in the society. With this conception of justice, individual, society state, government, nation and international organization moves from less just to more just for the sake of humankind.

Notes

1. Kant.*What is Enlightenment? in Kant on History*. p. 3.
2. *Ibid.,* p. 3.
3. Kant. *Enlightenment East and West.* p. 61.
4. Kamenka.*Justice*. p. 21.
5. Kant, *The Moral Law: Ground Work of The Metaphysic of Morals.* pp. 32-33.
6. *Ibid.,* p. 100-102.

Bibliography

Primary Sources

Hobbes, Thomas. *Leviathan.*Edited by Richard Tuck. UK: Cambridge University Press, 1991.

Hobbes, Thomas. *On the Citizen.* Edited by Richard Tuck, and translated by Michael SilVerthorne. UK: Cambridge University Press, 2003.

Kant, Immanuel. *The Moral Law: Groundwork of the Metaphysic of Morals.* Edited by H. J Paton. London: Hutchinson University Library). 1969.

Kant, Immanuel. *Groundwork of the Metaphysic of Morals.*Edited by LewisWhite Beck. Indianapolis IN: Bobbs-Merrill, 1959.

Kant, Immanuel. *Critique of Judgment,* Translated by Welner S Pulhar. New York: Indianapolis, 1987.

Kant, Immanuel. *Critique of Practical Reason.*Translated by L.W. Beck. New York: Liberal Arts Press, 1956.

Kant, Immanuel. *Critique of Practical Reason.*Translated by T. K. Abott. London: Longmans, Sixth edition, 1909.

Kant, Immanuel. *Doctrine of Virtue, Part II of the Metaphysic of Morals.* Translated by Mary J. Gregor. New York: Marker & Row Publishers, 1964.

Kant, Immanuel. *Perpetual Peace.*Edited by Lewis White Beck.Indianapolis: The Bobbs-Merrill Company Inc. 1967.

Kant, Immanuel. *Perpetual Peace: A Philosophical Essay.* Smith M Campbell. London: George Allen and Unwin Ltd, 1917.

Kant, Immanuel, *Enlightenment East and West.* Translated by Paulos Mar Gregorious. Delhi: B. R. Publishing, 1989.

Kant, Immanuel. *What is Enlightenment? in Kant on History.* Translated by Lewis White Beck. New York: Indianapolis, 1963.

Kant, Immanuel. "An Answer to the Question: What Is Enlightenment? (1784)", *What is enlightenment Eighteenth-Century Answers and Twentieth-Century Questions.* Edited by James Schmidt. 58-64. London: University of California Press. 1996.

Kant, Immanuel. 1790. *Science of Right.* Translated by W. Hasti. *e-Books Adelaide 2009.*

Kant, Immanuel. *Fundamental Principle of the Metaphysic of Ethics*. Translated by T.K. Abbot. Kings mill: Thomas Orient Publication, 1987.

Kant, Immanuel. *Doctrine of Virtue*. Translated by Gregar, Mary Philadelphia. London: University of Pennsylvana Press, 1964.

Kant, Immanuel. *Practical Philosophy*. Edited by M. Gregor. U.K: Cambridge University Press, 1996.

Kant, *Rechtslehre Einleitung*, p. 40, Quatation taken from Vaughan, C.E. *Studies in the history of Political Philosophy before and After Rousseau*. Manchester: Manchester University Press. 1939.

Kant, Immanuel. *The Metaphysical Principles of Virtue.* Translated by James Ellington. New York: Bobbs-Merrill Co., 1964.

Kant, Immanuel. *Metaphysic of Experience.* H. J. Paton. Volume 2, London: George Alleln & Unwin Ltd, 1961.

Kant, Immanuel, *What is Enlightenment? An Answer to the Question: "What is Enlightenment?"* Konigsberg in Prussia, 30th September 1784.

Locke, John. *An Essay Concerning Human Understanding*. Edited by Pattison, A.S. Pringle-Pattison. Oxford: The Clarendon Press. 1924.

Locke, John. *First Treatise on Civil Government*. Edited by Richard Ashcraft. London: Rutledge University Press, 1991.

Locke. John. *Two Treatise of Government*. Edited by Laslett Peter. U.K: Cambridge University Press, 1960.

Locke, John. *The Second Treatise of Government*. Edited by Perdon, P. Thomas. New York: The Liberal Arts Press, 1952.

Locke, John. *A Latter on Toleration*. Translated by J. W. Gough. Oxford: Clarendon press, 1968.

Rousseau, Jacques Jean. *The Social Contract*. Translated by Maurice Cranston. England: Penguin Books Limited, 1968.

Secondary Sources

Andrea T. Baumeister. *Liberalism and the Politics of Difference.* Edinbergh: Edinbergh University Press, 2000.

Aristotle, *Nicomachean Ethics*, Translated by H. Rackham, edited by. Jeffrey Henderson. Cambridge: Harvard University Press, 2003.

Aristotle. *The Nichomachean Ethics*. Translated by J.A.K. Thomson. U.K: Penguin Books, 2004.

Audi, Robert. *Practical Reasoning*. London and New York: Routledge, 1989.

Beck, L.W. ed. *Proceedings of the Third International Kant Congress*. Dordrecht-Holland: D. Reidel Publishing Company, 1972.

Beck, Lewis White. *A Commentary on Kant's Critique of Practical Reason*. Chicago: Chicago University Press, 1960.

Brian Barry. *A Treatise on Social justice volume II Justice as Impartiality*. Oxford: Clarendon Press. 2002.

Guyer, Paul. *Kant*. USA: Routledge, 2006.

Irwin Edman. *The Works of Plato*. Translated by Benjamin Jowett. UK: The Modern Library, 1965.

James P. Sterba. *Justice: Alternative Political Perspectives*. Canada: Wodswort/ Thomson Learning, 2003.

Johnston, David, "Kant's Theory of Justice," *A Brief History of justice*. Edited by David Johnston. 143-165. United Kingdom: Willy Blackwell, 2011.

Jr. Hill E Thomas, ed. *The Blackwell Guide to Kant's Ethics*. U.K: Blackwell Publishing Ltd., 2009.

Kamenka, Eugene. "What is justice?" *Ideas and Ideologies Justice.* Edited by Eugene Kamenka. 12. London: Edward Arnold Ltd., 1979.

Korsgaard, Christine M. *The Sources of Normativity*. Cambridge: Cambridge University Press, 1996.

Kuehn, Manfred, *Kant a Biography*. UK: Cambridge University Press, 2001.

Levine, Andrew. *The General Will: Rousseau, Marx, communism*. USA: Cambridge University Press, 1993.

Nussbaum, C Martha. "Social Contract and Three Unsolved Problems of Justice," *Frontiers of Justice Disability, Nationality, Species Membership.* Martha C Nussbaum. 09-99. New Delhi: Oxford University Press.

Mater D Roger. *The Political philosophy of Rousseau*. New Jersey: Princeton University Press, 1968.

Mill, Stuart John. *Utilitarianism*. New York: Liberal Arts Press, 1953.

..............., *Utilitariansim*. Indianapolis: Bobbs-Merill, 1957.

..............., *Utilitarianismon Liberty and Other Essays*. editedby John Gray Oxford: OUP, 1991.

Nisbet, H Reiss. tr. *Theories and Praxis in Kant's Political Writing*. Oxford: Blackwell. 1955.

O'Neill, Onora. *Constructions of Reason: Explorations of Kant's Practical Philosophy.* USA: Cambridge University Press, 1989.

Onarao'Neill, *Constructions of Reason: Explorations of Kant's Practical Philosophy*. USA: Cambridge University Press, 1989.

Plato, *Republic.* Translated by Desmond Lee. England: Penguin Groups. 1987.

Rosen. D. Allen. *Kant's Theory of Justice*. Itchaca: Cornell U.P. 1993.

Ross, W. D. The Right and the Good, Oxford: Clarendon Press, 1930.

Rawls, John. *A Theory of Justice*. Oxford: Clarendon Press, 1972.

Rawls, John. *The Law of Peoples*. Cambridge: Harvard University Press, 1999.

Russell, Bertrand. *A History of Western Philosophy*. New York: Simon and Schuster, 1945.

Sandel, J. Michael. *Liberalism and the Limits of Justice*. USA: Cambridge University Press, 1998.

Schmidt, James. "On the Question What is Enlightenment"? *What Is Enlightenment? Eighteenth Century Answers and Twentieth-Century Questions*. edited by Moses Mendelssohn. 53-57. London: University of California Press, 1996.

......................, "Introduction: What is Enlightenment? A Question, Its Context and Some Consequences," *What Is Enlightenment? Eighteenth Century Answers and Twentieth-Century Questions*.edited by James Schmidt. 144. London: University of California Press, 1996.

......................, "Public Use of Reason," *What Is Enlightenment? Eighteenth Century Answers and Twentieth-Century Questions*.edited by Earnest Ferdinand Klein. 85-144. London: University of California Press, 1996.

......................, "Autonomy, Individuality and Self Determination," *What Is Enlightenment? Eighteenth Century Answers and Twentieth-Century Questions*. edited by Lewis Hinchman. 448-517. London: University of California Press, 1996.

Sen, Amartya. *The idea of Justice*. London: Allen Lane, 2009.

Singh, R P. *Freedom and Causation with Special Reference to Hegel's Overcoming of Kant*. New Delhi: Om Publications, 2000.

Singh, RP. *Kant and Hegel Methodology, Ontology, Epistemology and Dialectic*. New Delhi: Galaxy Publication, 1990.

Singh, R.P. *A Critical Examination of Immanuel Kant's Philosophy*. New Delhi: Intellectual Publishing House, 1987.

Singh, R.P. *Dialectic of Reason*. New Delhi: Intellectual Publishing House, 1995.

Articles

Andrew, J. Reck. "The Enlightenment in American Law III: The Bill of Rights," *The Review of Metaphysics* 45, no. 1, 1991: 57-87, Accessed: 05/01/2012.

Antoon.Braeckman, "The Moral Inevitability of Enlightenment and the Precariousness of the Moment: Reading Kant's "What Is Enlightenment?," *The Review of Metaphysics* 62, no. 2, 2008: 285-306, Accessed: 15/04/2012.

Barnett, E. Randy. "A Consent Theory of Contract". *Columbia Law Review* 86, no. 2, 1986: 269-321. Accessed: 10/01/2012.

Beck, W. Lewis. "Kant and the Right of Revolution," *Journal of the History of Ideas* 32, no. 3 1971: 411-422, Accessed: 15/04/2012.

Benjamin, Radcliff. "The General Will and Social Choice Theory," *The Review of Politics* 54, no. 1, 1992: 34-49, Accessed: 10/01/2012.

Bookman T John. "Locke's Contract: Would People Consent to It"? *American Journal of Economics and Sociology* 43, no. 3, 1984: 357-368, Accessed: 10/01/2012.

Cohen, R. Morris. "The Basis of Contract". *Harvard Law Review* 46, no. 4, 1933: 553-592. Accessed: 10/01/2012.

Cormick, Mc Peter. "Social Contract: Interpretation and Misinterpretation," *Canadian Journal of Political Science* 9, no. 1, 1976: 63-76, Accessed: 10/01/2012.

Crowder, George. "Two Concepts of Liberal Pluralism," *Political Theory* 35, no. 2, 2007: 121-146, Accessed: 15/04/2012.

Curti, Merle. "The Great Mr. Locke: America's Philosopher 1783-1861". *The Huntington Library Bulletin*, no. 11, 1937: 107-151. Accessed: 05/01/2012.

David, Gauthier. "The Social Contract as Ideology", *Philosophy & Public Affairs* 6, no. 2, 1977: 130-164, Accessed: 10/01/2012.

Deveaux, Monique "Toleration and Respect", Public Affairs Quarterly, Vol. 12, No. 4, 1998, pp. 407-427, Accessed: 15/04/2012.

Edward A Harris. "From Social Contract to Hypothetical Agreement: Consent and the Obligation to Obey the Law," *Columbia Law Review* 92, no. 3, 1992: 651-683, Accessed 10/01/2012.

Franceschet, Antonio. "Sovereignty and Freedom: Immanuel Kant's Liberal Internationalist 'Legacy," *Review of International Studies* 27, no. 2, 2001: 209-22, Accessed: 15/04/2012.

Francis, Edward Devine. "Absolute Democracy or Indefeasible Right: Hobbes Versus Locke", *The Journal of Politics* 37, no. 3, 1975: 736-768. Accessed: 05/01/2012.

Freeman, Samuel "Reason and Agreement in Social Contract Views," *Philosophy & Public Affairs* 19, no. 2, 1990: 122-157.Accessed: 10/01/2012.

Harpham, Galt Geoffrey. "So What Is Enlightenment? An Inquisition into Modernity," *Critical Inquiry* 20, no. 3, 1994: 524-556, Accessed: 15/04/2012.

Harris, A. Edward. "From Social Contract to Hypothetical Agreement: Consent and the Obligation to Obey the Law". *Columbia Law Review* 92, no. 3, 1992: 651-683, Accessed: 10/01/2012.

Haydn, Mason. "The European Enlightenment: Was It Enlightened?," *The Modern Language Review* 94, no. 4, 1999: pp. xxvii-xxxviii, Accessed: 15/04/2012.

Herman, Lebovics. "The Uses of America in Locke's Second Treatise of Government," *Journal of the History of Ideas* 47, no. 4, 1986: 567-581.Accessed: 05/01/2012.

Herman, Lebovies. "The Uses of America in Locke's Second Treatise of Government," *Journal of the History of Ideas* 47, no. 4, 1986: 567-581, Accessed: 05/01/2012.

Huntley, L Wade. "Kant's Third Image: Systemic Sources of the Liberal Peace," *International Studies Quarterly* 40, no. 1, 1996: 45-76, Accessed: 15/04/2012.

Jeffrey, Reiman. "Towards a Secular Lockean Liberalism," *The Review of Politics*. 67, no. 3 2005: 473-493, Accessed: 05/01/2012.

Kemp, J. "Kant's Examples of the Categorical Imperative," *The Philosophical Quarterly* 8, no. 30, 1958: 63-71, Accessed: 02/06/2012.

L. Shannon Jung, "Autonomy as Justice: Spatiality and the Revelation of Otherness," *The Journal of Religious Ethics* 14, no. 1, 1986: 157-183, Accessed: 15/04/2012.

Ladenson, F Robert. "A Theory of Personal Autonomy," *Ethics* 86, no. 1, 1975: 30-48, Accessed 15/04/2012.

Lakoff, Sanford, "Autonomy and Liberal Democracy," *The Review of Politics* 52, no. 3, 1990: 378-396, Accessed: 15/04/2012.

Larry M. Preston, "Recovering the Social Contract by Ron Replogle." *The American Political Science Review* 84, no. 2, 1990: 640-641, Accessed: 10/01/2012.

Lewis, D H. "Is There a Social Contract? I", *Philosophy* 15, no. 57, 1940: 64-79, Accessed: 10/01/2012.

Lewis, D H. "Is There a Social Contract? II", *Philosophy* 15, no. 58, 1940: 177-189, Accessed: 10/01/2012.

Lewis, D H. "The Original Contract", *Ethics* 50, no. 2, 1940: 193-205, Accessed: 10/01/2012.

Micah, Schwartzman. "The Relevance of Locke's Religious Arguments for Toleration," *Political Theory* 33, no. 5, 2005: 678-705, Accessed: 10/01/2012.

Michael, Keeley. "Continuing the Social Contract Tradition", *Business Ethics Quarterly* 5, no. 2, 1995: 241-255, Accessed: 10/01/2012.

Murphy G Jeffrie. "Hume and Kant on the Social Contract", *Philosophical Studies: An International Journal for Philosophy in the Analytic Tradition* 33, no.1, 1978: 65-79, Accessed: 10/01/2012.

Murphy, G Jeffrie. "Kalin on the Categorical Imperative," *Ethics* 79, no. 2, 1969: 163-164, Accessed: 02/06/2012.

Myers, C Peter. "Between Divine and Human Sovereignty: The State of Nature and the Basis of Locke's Political Thought," *Polity* 27, no. 4, 1995: 629-649, Accessed: 05/01/2012.

Noone, John B. Jr. "The Social Contract and the Idea of Sovereignty in Rousseau", *The Journal of Politics* 32, no. 3, 1970: 696-708, Accessed: 10/01/2012.

Peterson, Jonathon. Enlightenment and Freedom.*Journal of the History of Philosophy* 46, no. 2, 2008: 223–44.

Reck, J Andrew. "The Enlightenment in American Law III: The Bill of Rights," *The Review of Metaphysics* 45, no. 1, 1991: 57-87, Accessed: 15/04/2012.

Rein'l, L Robert. "Comparative Philosophy and Intellectual Tolerance," *Philosophy East and West* 2, no. 4, 1953: 333-339, Accessed: 15/04/2012.

Robert A Holland. "A Theory of Establishment Clause Adjudication: Individualism, Social Contract, and the Significance of Coercion in Identifying Threats to Religious Liberty". *California Law Review* 80, no. 6, 1992: 1595-1694, Accessed: 05/01/2012.

Ruth, W. Grant. "Locke's Political Anthropology and Lockean Individualism," *The Journal of Politics* 50, no. 1, 1988: 42-63, Accessed: 05/01/2012.

Schossberger, Cynthia "Raising a question: Coercion and Toleration in Kant's Politics", *Ethics, Florianopolis* 5, no. 2, 2006: 165-171. 11/01/2012.

Scott, T John. "Politics as the Imitation of the Divine in Rousseau's "Social Contract", *Polity* 26, no. 3, 1994: 473-501, Accessed: 10/01/2012.

Scott, T John. "Politics as the Imitation of the Divine in Rousseau's Social Contract," *Polity* 26, no. 3, 1994: 473-501, Accessed: 10/01/2012.

Sonenscher, Michael. "Enlightenment and Revolution," *The Journal of Modern History* 70, no. 2, 1998: 371-383, Accessed: 15/04/2012.

Stacey, Simon. "A Lockean Approach to Transitional Justice," *The Review of Politics* 66, no. 1, 2004: 55-81, Accessed: 05/01/2012.

Strum, Arthur. "What Enlightenment Is," *New German Critique*, no. 79, Special Issue on Eighteenth-Century Literature and Thought, 2000: 106-136, Accessed. 15/04/2012.

Taylor, S Robert. "Kantian Personal Autonomy," *Political Theory* 33, no. 5, 2005: 602-628, Accessed: 15/04/2012.

Index

J

K

L

S

T